Divergences
Architecture in Latin America
and Discourses of the End of
the Century

Ingrid Quintana-Guerrero
Editor

Latin America: Thoughts

Romano Guerra Editora
Nhamerica Platform

Editors-in-Chief
Abilio Guerra
Fernando Luiz Lara
Silvana Romano Santos

Management Coordination
Fernando Luiz Lara
Irene Nagashima
Silvana Romano Santos

Divergences
Architecture in Latin America and
Discourses of the End of the Century
Ingrid Quintana-Guerrero (Editor)

BRA + USA + COL 11

Graphic Design and Formatting
Dárkon V Roque

Translation
Carolina Rodríguez
David Stevenson

Translation Review
Beatriz Lara
Noemi Zein Telles

Romano Guerra Editora
Nhamerica Platform
Universidad de los Andes

São Paulo, Austin,
Bogotá, 2024
1st edition

Divergences

Architecture in Latin America and Discourses of the End of the Century

Ingrid Quintana-Guerrero
Editor

Contents

06 Presentation
Latin America in Coexistence: Deciphering an Architectural Ethos
Ingrid Quintana-Guerrero

18 **Divergent Postmodernism: Waisman and Rossi's Thoughts in the Latin American Architectural Discourse**
Ingrid Quintana-Guerrero

40 **The Eighties: Other Architectures from Medellín, Colombia**
David Vélez Santamaría

64 **New Again: Contemporary Dialogues with Architectural Modernity in Latin America**
Ivo Giroto

96 **Pacific: Local Materialities and Transatlantic Perspectives**
Ingrid Quintana-Guerrero

122 **Materializing Imaginaries: Local Knowledge and Idiosyncrasies**
Ingrid Quintana-Guerrero

146 **Third-Nature Architecture for the Solidarity Landscape of the Interior in Mexico: an Approach from its Contemporaneity**
Fabricio Lázaro Villaverde
Edith Cota Castillejos

168 Post Scriptum
Babbling in Latin American Architecture of the 21st Century
Ingrid Quintana-Guerrero

174 **Divergent Voices**

176 **Authors' Biographies**

178 **Credits**

Presentation
Latin America in Coexistence: Deciphering an Architectural Ethos
Ingrid Quintana-Guerrero

In 2019, I wrote a text called "One Latin America? Defining an Architectural Region in the Late 20th Century."[1] It questioned different architectural discourses on the idea of a unitary Latin America. Its wording was a first – and most likely naïve – approach to theoretical inquiry into Latin American architecture and, tacitly, to the decolonizing will that emerged from the attempt at a common intellectual construction, particularly during the 1980s. Decolonization is a subject that, in the last decade and through different perspectives, has been extensively studied in academic areas such as social sciences and humanities. Architecture has not been alien to its emancipatory call either. However, the use and abuse of this term endanger simplifying its challenges and even reproducing colonialist patterns instead of eradicating them.[2]

Some authors have associated the processes of modernization with a colonizing drive, putting in crisis concepts articulated with architects' discourses and actions in the Latin American post-dictatorship period. In this spectrum, there is no room for negotiation with either Cristián Fernández Cox's "appropriate modernity"[3] or with Marina Waisman's plural postmodernities.[4] Remember that both Fernández Cox and Waisman were influential architectural thinkers at the time. Fernando Lara, alluding to Adrián Gorelik's definition of a Latin American city as a machine to invent modernity, questions: "Could modernity be appropriate if we had no choice but to accept it?"[5] His position seemed expected by the view of Francisco Liernur – who took part with Waisman in the major debates on Latin American thought during the 1980s – regarding the radical critique of Latin American modernity.

> Precisely because that condition [the onslaught against the Eurocentric canon] is accepted, it is usually opposed to the alleged naivety or clarity of the 'colonized', keeping the scheme of origin intact – and no less contaminated – and thereby recognizing the impossibility of any form of cultural resistance. The Euro-American modernist machine was so powerful that,

consistently and coherently, resisted any possibility of osmosis with the many cultures it has been encountering in its wake.[6]

The position that contemporarily recognizes osmosis, hybridization – García Canclini's concept, whose erroneous assimilation in architecture has been criticized by Felipe Hernández[7] –, and trans-modernity – according to Argentine Enrique Dussel – disengages in many moralizing (and polarizing!) academic works from the beginning of the second decade of the twenty-first century. It poses a fictitious situation. In the words of Silvia Rivera-Cusicanqui,[8] what happens in our territory is not a miscegenation but a coexistence of heterogeneous phenomena (around the colonizer and the colonized) that do not aspire to fuse nor produce new terms. However, considering that precolonial America was not homogeneous a priori, this coexistence (or overlap) of several *Latin Americas* might be the original condition of our subcontinent.

Amid the undeniable coexistence of multiple Latin American realities, and without detracting from the just claims of the indigenous' vindication in the intellectual and physical construction of our territory, negotiation is fundamental. This word, mainly in war conflict scenarios, implies tolerance and mutual surrender to achieve conciliation and avoid the oppressive tendency of those who Tuck and Wayne Yang[9] call "empowered postcolonial subjects."[10] In my opinion, this conciliatory attempt is present in most intellectual constructions of Latin American architecture, during the threshold of the immediate previous century. Many contemporary academics are not open today to this negotiation, under the pretext of repeating the colonizing cycle. However, it seems to me still necessary in the light of Santiago Castro-Gómez's thesis for whom "only by radicalizing universality, that is, universalizing its 'point of exclusion', can the decolonizing movement achieve its objectives."[11] Castro-Gómez's proposal implies a recognition of the vulnerability of the other, whether white, black, or indigenous, and of that which minimally reverberates from its ethos (despite Rivera's affirmation) in our current architectural thinking and making.

It is in this context of coexistence and negotiation, not only between native cultures and North Atlantic Treaty Organization – NATO-centric[12] doctrines but between diverse Latin American imaginaries that collide in sometimes violent and sometimes fortunate ways– that the architectural discourses enunciated in this book unfold. Given the scarcity of works that transversally address the discursive panorama of contemporary Latin American architecture, particularly in the twilight of the twentieth century,[13] my purpose as co-author and editor is to elaborate a retrospective and unsuspecting exercise from which, through divergent Latin American voices, common discursive lines emerge. Some of these are congruent with the spatial phenomena to which they are associated – revealing othernesses and vulnerabilities –, others are eager for redemption in the face of mistakes never repaired and privileges never abandoned – "moved towards innocence", in terms of Tuck and Wayne Yang.[14]

Necessary Clarifications on the Lines of Latin American Thought: Identity versus Ethos

I began by indicating my initial concern to understand the Latin-America concept in architecture, as a possible way to explain its processes of identity construction. Although I mentioned that the discussion is exhausted, I consider it necessary to establish a common basis for the reading of this work. Sometimes, it will be necessary to replace the word "identity" with "ethos" since the first inevitably refers to typical nationalist debates of the first decades of the twentieth century, while the second alludes to common characteristics, although less obvious, of our social DNA. An anthropophagic ethos, in the words of Falconi,[15] echoes the famous manifesto written by Oswald de Andrade in 1928. It is this diverse nature that accommodates the *architecture of divergence*, pointed out by Waisman in response to the architecture of *resistance* formulated by Kenneth Frampton, which allows us to understand as a multimodal region and not as a territory in which the relations of center and periphery prevail.[16] Additionally, it is necessary to think that some of these nodes operate as tentacles outside the Latin American physical territory and as inlets that penetrate it. According to Zeuler Lima "to continue to isolate Latin America as a geographic cluster and to attribute a unified identity to the architecture produced in it would mean to contradict its dynamism, multiplicity, and permeability [...]".[17]

Thinking about the *ethos* of contemporary Latin American architecture leads to identifying broad and flexible study categories. For example, Hugo Segawa[18] was interested in making regional contradictions visible through "lenses" such as landscape configuration, socially conscious technological development, introspective monumentality, and tropicalism confronted with barbarism. Horacio Torrent[19] did the same by rescuing perspectives left aside by the social approach of the Dependency Theory, such as inequality, poverty, and other Latin American dramas that sustain the spirit of place and the spirit of time discourses and macro-categories such as "monumentality" or "utopia and reality". Utopia as described by Ruth Verde Zein,[20] is not as a magic formula but as the belief and will that there is still the possibility of transforming the world into a better place, although in minuscule doses. Therefore, these would be more appropriate for a look at contemporary production. In his doctoral dissertation, Alexandre Ribeiro Gonçalves provides another transversal reading of this regional production (specifically that of the 1990s and 2000s), not from the projects' physical qualities but from the type of relationships between their multiple authors. For example, temporary associations, mentoring relationships, workshops, and other types of academic exchanges and participatory design, including users, where architects act as managers. These relationships inevitably affect what has been built and contribute to the constant development of our collective mentality as a subcontinental guild.

A final example of possible intellectual associations in recent regional architecture lies in the exhibition *Ethos de la arquitectura latinoamericana*.[21] Its curators – Silvia Arango, Jorge Ramírez Nieto, Ana Patricia Montoya, Rafael Méndez, and Ingrid Quintana-Guerrero – selected works based on three thematic areas – identity (understood not as consensus but as a framework for discussion on common phenomena), solidarity, and austerity. These subcategories describe situations and strategies that shape architecture instead of aesthetic features. Among them are the need to revitalize urban centers, recover cultural memory, create collective landmarks, temper spaces for comfort amid rigorous tropical heat and respond to rugged topographies. Many of the experiences included in the exhibition arise in urban contexts, whose heterogeneity and mutability are "divergent" from the architecture that populates Latin America, because of its contestatory and plural condition. In the words of Verde Zein "we try to understand, work and, as far as possible, appreciate our Latin American cities as they are – without the burden of heavy shadows of anachronistic conceptual ghosts unsuitable for the understanding of our realities."[22]

Divergences

Both the transnational associations proposed by *Ethos de la arquitectura latinoamericana* and those mentioned above focus on architectural works, from which the reader/viewer is led to the concept and, consequently, to the discourse. This finding was the starting point for the research collected in this book, no longer concentrating on materialized architectures but on the own and alien ideas that generate them. These contribute to the still scarce debate on the relationship between work and verbalized thought in Latin American architecture, inescapable within criticism. This study is preceded by a discursive analysis, limited to the Chilean territory, by Pedro Alonso, Umberto Bonomo, Macarena Cortés and Hugo Mondragón,[23] based on four thematic axes – form, art, place, and technique – represented as "subway lines" that intersect in specific stations (projects). Some of these axes will be discussed in the second part of this book.

In the next pages, we present two perspectives that promote the understanding of local phenomena and link spatially and geographically distant works. We organize these views in three transversal argument lines. The first examines the past through tools offered by architectural postmodernity, as a prelude to sharp and provocative reflections on the already controversial regional identity. The second aims to establish a global dialogue focused on materiality and form explorations. The third rrecognizes architectural culture emerged from the bottom up, fed by idiosyncrasies, ancestral knowledge adopted within the architectural technique, and collective architectural processes.

The first panoramic viewpoints include two chapters written by me. In "Divergent Postmodernism: Waisman and Rossi's Thoughts in the Latin American Architectural Discourse" I expose less visible reverberations compared to the reading of the Argentine architect on the theoretical production of Aldo Rossi in architectural writings from the 1980s and early 1990s, in Chile, Peru, and Paraguay.

In "Materialising Imaginaries. Local Knowledge and Idiosyncrasies" I discuss recent architectural practices that seek to vindicate Latin American architecture produced on the margins of "the formal", through the adaptation of ancestral knowledge and the translation of habits and meanings typical of the idiosyncrasy of those places where these practices take place. In no way should these sections be understood as an exhaustive and systematic study; on the contrary, they are cross-border inquiries in progress regarding the three lines of inquiry mentioned, which are susceptible to new interpretations, questioning, and refusing.

Adhering to this panoramic lens is "New Again: Contemporary Dialogues with Architectural Modernity in

Latin America" by Ivo Giroto. This text presents an intricate dialogue crossing between rupture and continuity, and divergence and convergence with the modern heritage. These were led by modern-trained masters and affirmed by the work of young architects throughout the region, mainly in Mexico and Brazil. Giroto discusses some changes and exchanges in the subcontinental contemporary architecture, through the analysis of important cultural facilities consolidated as preferential icons in a context of deepening neoliberal economic dynamics, competition between cities, and commodification of culture.

The second viewpoint provides an approach to these lines from three specific problems. The first of these texts is "The Eighties: Other Architectures from Medellín, Colombia" by David Vélez Santamaría. It offers an internationally unknown panorama of works built in the Colombian city, recognized worldwide for its past dominated by organized crime and, in its contemporary scenario, for operations that embody to the so-called "social urbanism". The architectures presented by Vélez led him to discuss relevant positions by their authors – associated with postmodern theories interpreted again under the lens of Marina Waisman. These, along with professional practice approaches on the discourses accompanying work dissemination and criticism at that time, went under the hypothesis that these works triggered the physical and social transformation of Medellín.

In the chapter "Pacific: Local Materialities and Transatlantic Perspectives", of my authorship, I question the argumentation for architectural action in the 1990s and early 2000s. This moved away from the doctrinal imposition on "the Latin American", in favor of recognizing universal concerns linked to the phenomenological, the symbolic landscape – particularly on the Pacific coast – and, of course, the foreign recognition of its contribution to the international architecture heritage with wide media coverage.

Finally, in "Third-Nature Architecture for the Solidarity Landscape of the Interior in Mexico. An Approach from its Contemporaneity" professors Fabricio Lázaro and Edith Cota identify and analyze six works and projects of Mexican emancipatory architecture, specifically from Oaxaca, Tijuana, San Luis Potosí, Baja California Norte, Chiapas, Puebla, and the State of Mexico. These works are from the second half of the twenty-first century, consolidating a practice that began on the threshold of the third millennium: the construction of third-nature collective frameworks. This is a term taken from Hannah Arendt, to describe the passage of adaptive action within the interior of the stressed crisis. With a strong critical accent, Lázaro and Cota point to the "glocal" inertia that resulted in pro-bono work by recognized offices, with the discourse of habitat management and social practice. They "seek balance in their media portfolios" and, in contrast, highlight actions of genuine interest because of their real contribution to social development.

To conclude, I must mention that this work was possible thanks to the Support Fund for Assistant Professors of the Vice-Rectory for Research and Creation, and the Faculty of Architecture and Design – ArqDis at the University of Los Andes – Uniandes, Colombia. I also acknowledge the work of the undergraduate assistants (today's colleagues) Angélica Luna, Isabela Cardona, and María Paula González who contributed to this research. The contribution and constant dialogue with countless colleagues were crucial, including those from the Observatory of Contemporary Latin American Architecture, and the academic network derived from the workshop "Nuestro Norte es el Sur" (Our North is the South) by the Global Architectural History Teaching Collaborative – GAHTC. Special gratitude to Ana María León of Harvard University for her pertinent bibliographic contributions and for helping me develop self-criticism with her sharp reflections and to my students of the undergraduate architecture course From the South: Thinking Architecture Today at ArqDis.

Notes

1. Presented at the 72nd annual conference of the Society of Architectural Historians, Providence (USA), April 25, 2019.
2. Tuck, Eve and K. Wayne Yang "La descolonización no es una metáfora." *Tabula Rasa*, no. 38 (2021): 61-111 <https://doi.org/10.25058/20112742.n38.04>.
3. Fernández Cox, Cristián. "Modernidad apropiada, modernidad revisada, modernidad reencantada." In *Modernidad y posmodernidad en América Latina: estado del debate*, edited by Cristián Fernández Cox and Enrique Browne, 99-109. Bogotá: Escala, 1991.
4. Waisman, Marina. "Las corrientes posmodernas vistas desde América Latina." Summa, no. 261 (1989): 44-47, 44.
5. Lara, Fernando Luiz. "Carta a mis amigos colombianos." *Dearq*, no. 29 (2021): 12-19 <https://doi.org/10.18389/dearq29.2021.02>, 13.
6. Liernur, Jorge Francisco. "¡Es el punto de vista, estúpido!" *Arqa*, 13 Dec. 2011 <https://arqa.com/actualidad/documentos/es-el-punto-de-vista-estupido.html>, n.p.
7. "The self-referentiality of the architectural discourse has rendered it incapable of grasping the complexity of the term. This could be the reason why hybridization has been mistaken as a finalizable process in opposition to the unfinalizability of the process of cultural becoming that it tries to represent. [...] In other words, the theoretical/anthropological facet of [García] Canclini's notion of hybridization addresses a series of socio-cultural problems in relation to the economy and market structures that exist in Latin America, in order to propose that new structures be created in the continent to compete in the global market." Hernández, Felipe. "On the Notion of Architectural Hybridisation in Latin America". *Journal of Architecture* 7, no. 1 (2002): 77-86 <https://doi.org/10.1080/13602360110114722>, n.p.
8. Rivera-Cusicanqui, Silvia. *Ch'ixinakax utxiwa: una reflexión sobre prácticas y discursos descolonizadores.* Buenos Aires: Tinta Limón, 2010.
9. Tuck and Wayne Yang, "La descolonización no es una metáfora," 85.

10. In reply, Tuck and Wayne Yang propose the term "incommensurability" understood as "[...] a recognition that decolonization will require a change in the order of the world. This is not to say that indigenous, black, or brown people adopt positions of domination over white settlers. The goal is not to just exchange places in the colonial triad of settlement, taking another turn in the same carousel. The purpose is to break the relentless structuring of the triad; a rupture and not a commitment." Ibid., 67.
11. Castro-Gómez, Santiago. "¿Qué hacer con los universalismos occidentales? Observaciones en torno al 'giro decolonial'." *Analecta Política* 7, no. 13 (2017): 249-272, 256.
12. Here I appropriate the concept proposed by Loredo Cansino, Reina, and Fernando Luiz Lara. "Introducción." In *Apuntes sobre decolonización, arquitectura y ciudad en las Américas*, edited by Reina Loredo Cansino y Fernando Luiz Lara, 27-48. Tamaulipas: Universidad Autónoma de Tamaulipas, 2020, 28.
13. As mentioned later in this book, these types of readings are usually local and focus on the first two decades of the twenty-first century. Amongst the rare attempts to group recent projects through discourse paradigm shifts are the work of Plaut, Jeannette and Marcelo Sarovic. *Pulso 2: nueva arquitectura en latinoamérica*. Santiago: Constructo, 2014, which compares common phenomena in different Latin American cities, and the cycle of conferences "Latitudes", organized by the Center for American Architecture and Design at the University of Texas between 2009 and 2015, which included hosts and guests from schools and architectural firms throughout the Americas.
14. Tuck and Wayne Yang, "La descolonización no es una metáfora," 66.
15. Falconi, José Luis. "No Me Token; or, How to Make Sure We Never Lose the * Completely." *Guggenheim UBS Map*, Perspectives, October 30, 2013 <https://www.guggenheim.org/blogs/map/no-me-tokenor-how-to-make-sure-wenever-lose-the-completely>.
16. Waisman, Marina. *El interior de la historia: historiografía arquitectónica para uso de latinoamericanos*. Bogotá: Escala, 1990, 64.
17. Lima, Zeuler R. "Architectural Developments in *Latin America: 1960-2010*." In *A Critical History of Contemporary Architecture: 1960-2010*, edited by Elie G. Haddad and David Rifkind, 163-187. London: Routledge, 2014, 176.

18. Segawa, Hugo. *Arquitectura latino-americana contemporánea.* Barcelona: Gustavo Gilli, 2005.
19. Torrent, Horacio. "Cristal opaco: la arquitectura latino-americana como categoría historiográfica." In *Sudamérica moderna,* edited by Hugo Modragón and Catalina Mejía, 276-290. Santiago: Ediciones ARQ, 2015, 285-288.
20. Verde Zein, Ruth. *O lugar da crítica: ensaios oportunos de arquitetura.* Porto Alegre: Editora Ritter dos Reis, 2010, 260.
21. Quintana-Guerrero, Ingrid, and Rafael Ernesto Méndez Cárdenas, eds. *Ethos de la arquitectura latinoamericana: identidad, solidaridad, austeridad. Memorias de una exposición.* Quito: Centro de Publicaciones de la Pontificia Universidad Católica del Ecuador, 2018.
22. Verde Zein, *O lugar da crítica,* 259. Translation by the editors.
23. Alonso, Pedro Ignacio, Umberto Bonomo, Macarena Cortés, and Hugo Mondragón. "El discurso de la arquitectura contemporánea chilena: cuatro debates fundamentales." *Rita: revista indexada de textos académicos,* no. 7 (2017): 54-59 <https://doi.org/10.24192/2386-7027(2017)(v7)(01)>.

Divergent Postmodernism: Waisman and Rossi's Thoughts in the Latin American Architectural Discourse
Ingrid Quintana-Guerrero

To resist is to maintain a situation, create your own enclave in the system to not be absorbed by it. To diverge is to develop from what one is, what one can become.
Marina Waisman, "Las corrientes postmodernas vistas desde América Latina"[1]

Introduction

In 2020, following the hundredth anniversary of the birth of the Argentine architect Marina Waisman (Buenos Aires, 1920 – Río Cuarto, 1997), the relevance of her thoughts about Latin American architecture resurged. This coincided with the Covid-19 pandemic, so several commemorations planned for the occasion did not play out. However, Waisman's name is still cited, critically or referentially, for theoretical and historical purposes when speaking on Latin American architecture.

Waisman was not an architect by "trade"; however, her theoretical work permeated into the design work of many of her contemporaries. This has been very much disputed,[2] particularly her role as a central figure at the Seminars of Latin American Architecture – SAL, where the first phase involved prominent architects committed to the construction of the "Latin American identity" through their work. Other notable members of SAL include Rogelio Salmona, Abraham Zabludovsky, and Severiano Porto. The junction of professionals and academics in the same discussion had a clear impact in Southern Cone's pedagogical and editorial experiences, from which various readings on architectural postmodernity were disseminated. In the text "Traduciendo a Rossi: de Buenos Aires a Nueva York," Ana María León identifies two areas of postmodern influence in Argentina – with repercussions in the rest of the region.[3] One focused on formal experimentation and the other on humanistic concerns. León links them to different interpretations of *L'architettura della città* from 1966 by Peter Eisenman and Marina Waisman. The following section expresses not only

Waisman's interpretation of Aldo Rossi but also the implications of this work for architectural thought during the 1980s and the early 1990s in three specific areas of South America.

Rossi from Waisman's Perspective

The editorial work of young Waisman in *Summa* – a magazine and publishing house in Buenos Aires where she worked from the beginning of the 1970s and directed the *Summarios* collection in 1976 –, was the main source of dissemination and critical analysis of Rossi's original texts. Around the same time, Aldo Rossi visited Argentina, as a guest of *La Escuelita*, between 1978 and 1982.[4] This Italian architect had generated magnetism in the local architectural guild, promoting a return to the city for an understanding of architectural typology as a historical artifact,[5] beyond just formal manipulation.[6] In *Summarios*, Waisman also published texts by another Italian, Manfredo Tafuri, to support the idea of typology as "a tool to connect architecture to society, rather than an isolating discipline with internal and autonomous processes."[7] In doing so, he accused Rossi's followers in the Southern Cone of making an abstract interpretation of the term "type" that was far from the author's original intention.

Indirectly, Argentine critics attacked the postmodern discourse developed in the United States, specifically in New York, based on Eisenman's reading of Rossi's work, stripping it "from all contexts and transformed, literally and figuratively, into an autonomous figure."[8] These views contrasted not only the interpretations but the contexts in which these interpretations were received – and provoked – and the demands made on the discipline. For example, repression was widespread in the Southern Cone because of various dictatorships,[9] while in the United States, economic growth and its consequences on consumption habits were remarkable.

A genuine concern for the "here" and "now" prompted *Summa* to recurrently publish projects committed to a vision of postmodernity that exceeded the discipline's limits and established strong links with history, including the work of Argentines such as Clorindo Testa, and Miguel Ángel Roca. Despite the economic crisis at the end of Jorge Videla's dictatorship in 1981, and the effects of the Falklands War, the local building production was considerably low. This was reflected in the magazine with the increase in critical and research articles.

Therefore, *Summa* expanded its gaze towards neighboring countries, both in its theoretical contents and in the selection of works and projects – many of which were never built. This established a network of designers linked to the SAL, starting in 1985 in Buenos Aires. Waisman's crusade to examine and disseminate Latin American postmodern architecture within the international context began, with a special concern to develop analytical categories.[10]

It was only until 1989 that Waisman, based in Córdoba, published a text in *Summa* that summarized her established reflections on what she called "Corrientes arquitectónicas vistas desde Latinoamérica" – architectural movements from the Latin America perspective. These lines critique the appropriation of postmodernity because "they drag [...] as a consequence of the general drive of the world,"[11] in a process similar to the establishment of a modern continental architecture. This statement anticipates the position adopted a year later by Fernández,[12] who understood postmodernity as a phenomenon alien to Latin America.

Waisman, however had been concerned with decoding and decanting the postmodern, but not condemning the *verborragia vacua* (empty verbosity) provoked by superficial interpretations of postmodern thought in the Americas, derived in eclecticisms, anachronistic collages, and epidermal folklores, which lost the true reason for being folklore: the participation of folk in its conception and execution.[13] These traits would be typical of transplanted ideological systems that, in the words of Alberto Petrina, alienate the relationship between theory and praxis.[14] As an alternative to the "architectures of silence" aroused by these interpretations, Waisman opposed the "architecture of the word," committed to social classes that had lost visibility as historical actors, by pluralism and a greater figuration of architecture in non-central countries.[15]

This 1989 article is one of the main antecedents for the publication of *La arquitectura descentrada* from 1995. It was there that Waisman introduced the notion of cultural *systems* as the foundation for a new postmodernity paradigm,[16] as "a set of subcultures submerged [not to say infiltrated] in dominant cultures."[17] In a brief text in *El interior de la historia*, from 1972, she introduced another crucial word: *fragmentation* (of universal historical narratives) in favor of the construction of multiple narratives.[18]

As a response to this last aspect and not wanting to settle "in the periphery" – form of resistance and cultural place away from the dominant culture and preferred by some Latin Americans[19] – Waisman opposed the recognition of an undergoing project – a divergent Latin American architecture – that circulated in specialized media outside the region. This included the article "Architectural Theory for Latin America," the catalog of the exhibition "10 Arquitectos Latinoamericanos," held in Seville in 1989, and several issues in the Spanish magazine *Arquitectura Viva*,[20] featuring the first edition of *Monografías A&V* from 1988, entirely dedicated to Latin America. Waisman stated that "resistance does not imply a project for the future, resistance is a project for the future, however difficult or improbable it may arise."[21]

The selection elaborated by Waisman throughout her transcontinental collaborations, particularly in *Monografías A&V*, included projects by authors from the SAL committed to that future project, such as Rogelio Salmona, Severiano Porto, Francisco de Assis Couto de Reis, and Edward Rojas. Other relevant works highlighted by Waisman in the European context were heritage interventions, reinforcing the interest in history fostered by the reading of the Italians. Besides Roca and Testa, she mentioned the Villanueva shopping center – retrofit of the Seminario Mayor de Medellín by Laureano Forero in 1982 – and the reconstruction of the Mercado Modelo in Salvador de Bahia, designed by Paulo de Azevedo in 1986.[22] It is striking that, despite questioning the center-periphery vision, this review includes only examples from the dominant countries in the regional historiography such as Argentina, Brazil, and Mexico; more recently, Uruguay, Colombia and Venezuela. At least half of the examples come from the Southern Cone.[23] This is a flaw of which she was fully aware, which persists in studies on late twentieth century architecture in Latin America[24] and to which these lines aim to contribute with three parallel cases.

Appropriate Postmodernity or After Postmodernism

Waisman's 1989 text and her subsequent articles in European journals are the product of mature processes and ideas that formed the complex mapping of Latin American architectural postmodern thought. Although her contribution to Latin American architectural theory in the late twentieth century has been addressed in regional historiography, the text addresses Chile of the early 1980s where, in parallel to the positioning of Rossi's perspective on Argentina, the syntactic approach of Latin American postmodernism was gaining strength and influencing its closest neighbors.[25] This was confirmed by a series of meetings with renowned figures of the international postmodern scene, such as Eisenman and Michael Graves, who were invited to the first Biennial of Santiago (1979), and Charles Moore, who attended the third version in 1981. Despite the language differences between the projects of the "New York's whites" and Moore's projects, the formal emphasis of these authors is recognised in several works presented in the following versions of Biennial of Santiago and the first versions of the SAL (1985 and 1986).

By the time of these biennials, magazines such as *ARS*, *ARQ* and *AUCA* had already highlighted the work of these authors, who, according to Pérez,[26] pioneered a "canonical postmodernism" in Chile (regarding Graves and Moore's work). Among these were different proposals for the national competition Nueva Santa Isabel (1976)[27] and the building Fundación (1982), both in Santiago.[28] Cristián Boza – architect of this building – had a vast corporate production, exemplifying a particular stage in Latin American architecture, where postmodernism as a style seemed to precede the deep discussions behind the notion of postmodernity.[29] Meanwhile, other young Chilean architects, such as Cristián Fernández,[30] began to show interest in experimental conceptual projects, for example, the church at the Seminario Pontificio de Santiago. The publication of this project in *ARS* marked a turning point – towards maturity – not only for the magazine but also for the direction that Chilean architecture was taking.[31]

The fourth version of Santiago's biennials in 1983 embraced even more theoretical discussions, taking a turn towards Waisman's regionalist position on postmodernity. This was materialized with the parallel organization of the Taller América by Fernández Cox – an academic and practicing architect, who would later become one of the most active participants of the SAL. The abandonment of canonical postmodern architecture as the center of discussions also impacted the aforementioned publications, which by the 1980s[32] were promoting a pro-modern left-wing stance.[33] Regional historiography has rarely cited another discussion scenario around this topic, which emerged during the same year in the fifth Biennial of Architecture in Lima (1983). There, Peruvian postmodern architecture was debated in public for the first time.[34] From the beginning, it was tailored following Tafuri and Rossi's interest in the historic city as the main input of architecture, which resonated in Waisman's texts.[35] In the Torres de Limatambo, opened in the Peruvian capital the same year of the fifth Biennial, the architects Óscar Borasino, Manuel Ferreyra, Juan Gutiérrez, Diego La Rosa, Hugo Romero, and Reynaldo Ledgard designed one of the first urban operations of postmodernity in Lima. These

Torres de Limatambo (Lima, 1983).
Borasino, Ferreyra, Gutiérrez, La Rosa,
Romero and Ledgard

Source: Ingrid Quintana-Guerrero, 2019.

operations used elements of the colonial urban structure, such as the street and the block, to create a matrix on which modern housing blocks were placed, connected by a network of diagonal pedestrian paths.[36]

Ledgard had been one precursor of postmodern architectural thought in Peru. His perspective was more Anglo-Saxon compared to the one guiding the conception of Torres de Limatambo, a project inspired not only by Rossi but also by Leon Krier, and London's Royal Mint Square Housing project in 1974. In a text published in the local magazine *Habitat* (1983), he endorsed Venturi's *Complexity and Contradiction in Architecture*, as well as in his article "A soft manifesto in favor of an equivocal architecture."[37] In contrast, projects such as Juan Carlos Domenack's La Fontana Shopping Centre appeared as a literal echo of Graves' architecture, confirming Domenack's interest in his work. "It is

Centro cultural Miraflores (Lima, 1992). Juan Carlos Doblado, José Orrego and Javier Artadi

Source: Ingrid Quintana-Guerrero, 2019.

about attacking the mediocrity and hypocrisy of the environment – according to the designers – and proposing architecture as a means to avoid them."[38] According to the architect and researcher José Beingolea del Carpio, the application of postmodern formal mechanisms was validated in Lima, regardless of their theoretical origin. Although, it is almost certain that Waisman's historical and taxonomic vision rested (and prevailed) behind these strategies.

In Ledgard's case, his adherence to the Venturian postulates was based, to some extent, on a series of articles published by Augusto Ortiz de Zevallos a year earlier in the magazine *Debate*, titled "Down with functionalism. And up with what?". Here he warned that "current fashion should not cloud the vision that most of the supposedly contestatory architecture, which today claims to be postmodernist, is [*sic*] historically blind and formally reactionary,"[39] which "echoes the typically postmodern plurality and eclecticism."[40] Despite these comments, Peru in the 80s was an epicenter of the regional turn claimed by Waisman and reinforced by Chabuca Granda (1983-1985), another important housing project in the center of Lima by Jorge García Bryce. Here García Bryce proposed both a typological reading and a historicist aesthetic through ornaments that recreate traditional elements of Peruvian popular architecture. However, the architect's conceptual reference was from Europe, more precisely from the *Internationale Bauausstellung* (IBA) in

Chabuca Granda Housing Project (Lima, 1983-195). Jorge García Bryce

Source: Ingrid Quintana-Guerrero, 2019.

Berlin, which included Rossi and Krier (among other prominent names), and which general plan started from the block as a basic projection unit.[41] Other proposals were the headquarters of the Banco Mercantil also by García Bryce and San Francisco square's houses by José Carlos Barrenechea.[42]

Dichotomous Postmodernities

Enrique Browne's work mediates between the symbolic and historical lenses of postmodernism.[43] His projects adopt a heterogeneous language – some of his most recognised buildings have a certain *high-tech* affiliation[44] –, while his theoretical framework dialogues with central themes of the Taller América and the SAL – which he was part of. In *Otra*

Consorcio Vida Building (Santiago, 1993). Enrique Browne and Borja Huidobro
Source: Ingrid Quintana-Guerrero, 2019.

arquitectura en América Latina (1988), Browne responds to Fernández Cox's call in 1990 to avoid the search for "surnames" to characterize Latin American modernity or postmodernity. These end up suggesting the irremediable disappointment of what the second author refers to as "illustrated postmodernity" – the "symbolic", in Doblado's words already cited, or "canonical", in ours words.

Consequently, the connection between Browne's works and his writings is not direct, since the latter allude, mainly, to urban issues and an examination of his peers' production[45] around a narrative about the "spirit of the time" and the "spirit of the place". The latter echoed the critical regionalism proclaimed by Kenneth Frampton[46] in 1983, with which Browne reaffirmed a rupture between the architecture "of development" – or international architecture, to which his work seemed to affiliate following the "spirit of the time" – and the "other architecture" or "creole"[47] in the words of García "which is in deep dialogue with its place."[48] The dichotomy singularly embodied by Browne's work, in different degrees, permeated other countries in the region, where discourse and work seemed to walk along distant lines of the same path called Postmodern Architecture.

For example, this dichotomous condition was known in the Guarani context some years later. Paraguay has only recently begun to appear in regional historiography for issues outside postmodernism; although, due to a contemporary production of wide international recognition that is conceptually established within postmodernity.[49] The work of relevant architects of the 1970s and 1980s, such as Genaro "Pindú" Espínola or Silvio Feliciángeli was based on the semiology exhibited by the Italian philosopher and art historian Gillo Dorfles in his essay *Symbol, Communication and Consumption* from 1975.[50] Meanwhile, another group of Paraguayan professionals were dialoguing with local living traditions, using language influenced by Robert Venturi and Denisse Scott-Brown's production.

The first architects – including local professionals such as Carlos Cabo de Vila, Carlos Cataldi and Mirta Lemir – adhered to what Morra called the "reductionist process" of the form.[51]

They used deliberate gestures consistent with the understanding of architectural elements as signifiers, which led to a strong symbolization in works such as the Nautilus or the Curupayty I buildings. The second group of architects established this dialogue and local affirmation within a very similar language to that of their contemporaries, but recovering the value of the popular domestic typology, *culata jovai*, with intermediate spaces that integrate the inside and outside. According to Morra, this decision would be protected by the inescapable assumption of the street as a physical and meaningful reality and in the context produced by tall new buildings in Asunción –"urban elements magnified in their scale."[52] Many of these were public buildings erected during the last phase of Alfredo Stroessner's dictatorship, which could not solve their "front and back" in the best way, causing irreversible changes in the urban morphology of the Paraguayan capital. The position of this second group would also be protected by the Venturian premise that "architecture occurs in the meeting of interior and exterior forces of use and space."[53] These internal and environmental

Nautilus Building (Asunción, 1988).
Genaro Espínola
Source: Ingrid Quintana-Guerrero, 2019.

Terrazas de Villa Morra Residential Building (Asunción, 1982). Silvio Feliciángeli

Source: Ingrid Quintana-Guerrero, 2019.

forces are general and particular; generic and circumstantial. Architecture as a wall between the interior and exterior is the spatial trace and the setting for this agreement. "Recognizing the difference between the interior and the exterior, architecture once again opens its doors to the urban point of view."[54]

The approach to the more Italian version of Rossi in Paraguayan architectural discourse also had a southern input, given the close relationship between the University of Córdoba in Argentina – where Waisman worked – and the nascent Catholic University of Nuestra Señora de Asunción – UC, founded in 1980 as a reaction to official doctrines

– related to a modernist aesthetic – promoted by Faculty of Architecture, Design and Art of The Asunción Nacional University – FADA UNA.[55] The architects Luis Alberto Boh and Christian Andersen relied on the model from Córdoba to create this new school, with the input of Pablo Cappelletti, renowned architect within Asunción's architectural sphere. This later helped to renew FADA UNA's teaching staff, which trained professionals who develop a new architectural stand regarding the city in Asunción, through the unprecedented lens of its human condition, so demanded by Aldo Rossi.[56] Echoing the "spirit of place and time" proclaimed by Browne, Morra stated that a "decisive spiritual reaction between us and our places, between our way of building"[57] was necessary for Asunción in Paraguay to face the situation denounced by the Italian architect. Therefore, taking pre-existences into account and using typological elements was more sophisticated in quality domestic projects by Boh, Víctor González and Annie Granada, among others,[58] even with a postmodern language.

The relationship between a new generation of Paraguayan architects with Rossi, Tafuri, Giancarlo DiCarlo and other professionals from the Venetian School did not require Waisman's intellectual mediation. According to Verri Lopes,[59] young architects introduced as teachers by Capelletti to the UNA, had the opportunity to travel to Italy to study postgraduate courses – such as Javier Corvalán who specialized in urban center recovery. This opened a door for the exchange of teachers and students from Paraguay and the Istituto Universitario d'Architettura di Venezia, as well as the discussion of the ideas between both schools. This dialogue, influenced by the aftermath of the famous exhibition La Presenza del Passato at the Biennale de Venezia in 1980,[60] was consolidated years later with the repeated participation of Paraguayans in academic and curatorial activities in Venice. Those exhibited architecture defined as being from the *inmundo* (i.e., outside the Western canons, at the end of the world).[61] This is an architecture of divergence.

According to Fernández Cox, it proposes languages and processes that lack any surname related to foreign intellectual movements, or with those terms coined at the SAL and validated by Waisman's analysis, even when they engage in a critical dialogue.

Coda

Although the circulation of Waisman's texts was wide, it was restricted for several years by constraints related to physical media (e.g., reduced circulation of copies, slow home delivery systems, dissemination restricted to specific circles of professionals), and by the impossibility of freely accessing academic information, in countries still governed by dictatorships during the second half of the 1980s. Therefore, this text should be understood not as an attempt to trace this operation but to identify the influences of these thoughts – particularly the interpretation of Rossi. This influence was discreet in less visible regional studies marked by the imprint of the SAL, thanks to the circulation of ideas and actors in the professional and academic fields, which contrasts with the intense media coverage of the Anglo-Saxon postmodern work.

This exercise requires a broader examination in areas in which postmodernity in architecture has been less generalized – Brazil is perhaps the most representative case, with little attention paid to postmodern production in states such as Amazonas and Minas Gerais. However, these areas were not immune to Waisman's ideas – and, indirectly, of Rossi's – in the voice of critics, researchers, and architects outside the local mainstream.

Notes

1. Waisman, Marina. "Las corrientes posmodernas vistas desde América Latina." *Summa*, no. 261 (1989): 44-47, 47.
2. Among the works that have addressed this issue are Zambrano Torres, María Rosa. "Corrientes posmodernas vistas desde América Latina: la arquitectura 'latinoamericana' en la crítica arquitectónica de Marina Waisman." *Rita: revista indexada de textos académicos*, no. 4 (2015): 152-159 <http://ojs.redfundamentos.com/index.php/rita/article/view/82/8> and Souza, Gisela Barcellos de. "Tessituras híbridas ou o duplo regresso: encontros latino-americanos e traduções culturais do debate sobre o retorno à cidade." PhD diss., Universidade de São Paulo, 2013 <https://teses.usp.br/teses/disponiveis/16/16133/tde-12072013-111253/publico/GISELA_BARCELLOS_TESE.pdf>.
3. León, Ana María. "Traduciendo a Rossi: de Buenos Aires a Nueva York." *PLOT*, no. 8 (2012): 218-21.
4. "Banned from teaching at the university, the architects [Tony Díaz, Ernesto Katzenstein, Justo Solsona and Rafael Viñoly, who collaborated in *Summa*] came together to create an institution of their own. However, as the political situation deteriorated and a military junta took over the city, the project began to change [...] Operating within a charged political atmosphere, the discourse of La Escuelita pointed to the potential for action within the discipline. This idea — that the architect should be a part of a broader cultural, intellectual, and political milieu, and that architecture itself should reclaim the city as a site — was the strongest memory Rossi left behind in Buenos Aires." León, Ana María. "Aldo Rossi: La Escuelita, Buenos Aires, Argentina, 1976-1983." Radical Pedagogies, n.d.
5. León states the following about the more "exemplary" reading of the concept "type" made by Waisman, much closer to Giulio Carlo Argan's theory: "Waisman's overdetermined typological taxonomies were precisely the kind of classification that post-structuralism was interested in destabilizing. [...] By erasing Rossi from the discussion of the type, Waisman attempted to open a space for the use of typology in an architecture that is still seen as modern, and thus delay the most historicist or autonomous tendencies of postmodernism [...] in contrast to Waisman's defense against excessive formalisms or historicisms, Eisenman aspired to a modernity that the discipline had never had, that is, a modernity based on the internal processes of the form." León, "Traduciendo a Rossi".
6. León, "Aldo Rossi."
7. León, "Traduciendo a Rossi," 219.
8. Ibid., 218.
9. Ibid., 218.
10. Zambrano Torres, "Corrientes posmodernas vistas desde América Latina."

11. Waisman, "Las corrientes posmodernas vistas desde América Latina," 44.
12. Fernández Cox, Cristián. *Arquitectura y modernidad apropiada: tres aproximaciones y un intento.* Santiago: Taller América, 1990.
13. Corona Martínez, Alfonso. "Comentarios adicionales sobre el posmodernismo latinoamericano." *Summa* no.261 (1989): 48-50.
14. Despite the severity of the warning, Waisman's text (also published in *Summa*) Petrina stated: "Personally, postmodern currents don't worry me much or too much. I consider them completely outside our current cultural circumstance, and not only in the American space but also in time, because some of them have had such an ephemeral existence that they already belong to the past. On the other hand, I suspect that Marina does not worry either. Sometimes one must focus conjecturally on certain topics [...] to discuss them with colleagues in seminars and magazines, without anyone losing sleep about them." Petrina, Alberto. "Historia de una pasión racional." *Summa*, no. 261 (1989): 50-51.
15. Waisman, "Las corrientes posmodernas vistas desde América Latina."
16. Zambrano Torres, "Corrientes posmodernas vistas desde América Latina."
17. Waisman, "Las corrientes posmodernas vistas desde América Latina," 45.
18. Zambrano Torres, "Corrientes posmodernas vistas desde América Latina."
19. Corona Martínez, "Comentarios adicionales sobre el posmodernismo latino-americano."
20. Zambrano Torres, "Corrientes posmodernas vistas desde América Latina."
21. Waisman, "Las corrientes posmodernas vistas desde América Latina," 47.
22. Zambrano Torres, "Corrientes posmodernas vistas desde América Latina."
23. "This is not, of course, all Latin American architecture. But it is the one by which Latin America can be recognized as a significant cultural entity in the architecture of the world." Waisman, "Las corrientes posmodernas vistas desde América Latina," 47.
24. Except for Antonio Toca, Corona and Waisman's contributions, in *Summa* (as well as the mentioned examination that, regarding those contributions, was conducted by María Rosa Zambrano Torres), the revisions of the regional landscape of architectural postmodernity remain scarce. Those cited here correspond to local perspectives whose dialogue with other Latin American latitudes is reduced to Waisman's point of view. Adding to the scarce views of *Summa*'s collaborators is the collection "SomosSur" published by David Serna in Escala (Bogotá), between 1989 and 1994. Although its focus was broader, it included volumes dedicated to the work of Togo Díaz, Teodoro González de León, and Carlos Mijares, among others.

25. This is a partially true statement for the Bolivian case because I had restricted access to sources on this country's architecture during the Covid-19 pandemic. In any case, even locally the work is "invisible" and without registration, as mentioned: "Architectural production in Bolivia is strong, but among other causes, the absence of publications that record it has determined its invisibility within the Latin American architecture panorama. Its architects have also not cared enough to make themselves known local biennials are scarce (there have been only 11 in La Paz and four in Santa Cruz de la Sierra, in recent years). Additionally, no compilations have been produced and participation in other international events tends to be sporadic. The production of magazines or related prints depends almost exclusively on the colleges of architects' administration [...]". Díaz-Osorio, Myriam Stella. "Arquitectura latinoamericana contemporánea: arquitectura invisible en Bolivia." *Diseño en Síntesis*, no. 50-51 (October 2014): 50-65, 65.
26. Fernando Pérez Oyarzún, interview not published by Ingrid Quintana-Guerrero, 2019.
27. It was a pioneering initiative in the urban renewal of downtown Santiago, to develop the area south of the Avenue Bernardo O'Higgins, Santiago. Cf. Hernández González, Olivar, and María Rosa Giugliano Perellano. "Concurso nacional de arquitectura Nueva Santa Isabel." *AUCA: Arquitectura Urbanismo Construcción Arte*, no. 31 (2020): 6-10 <https://revistaauca.uchile.cl/index.php/AUCA/article/view/59503/62952>.
28. The project consisted of a 40-meters high building which language was inspired by the representative buildings of Santiago's center, with a solid marble facade with a superimposed 27-story tower covered with mirror glass. Cf. Boza, Cristián, Jorge Luhrs, and José Muzard. "Edificio Fundación." *AUCA: Arquitectura Urbanismo Construcción Arte*, no. 44 (1982): 36-37 <https://revistapolitica.uchile.cl/index.php/AUCA/article/view/59910>.
29. Doblado, Juan Carlos. "Influencia del posmodernismo en la arquitectura de Lima 1980-2000." Master Thesis, Universidad Nacional de Ingeniería, Lima, 2018, 39.
30. In the project's description, Fernández argued the antagonism between use ("functionalism") and meaning ("language"), promoted by the Argan's approach: "a church is an obvious manifestation of this: its use and meaning are so interpenetrated that it is often difficult to distinguish which one is being talked about." Fernández Cox, Cristián. "Teoría y práctica: iglesia del seminario pontificio de Santiago." *ARQ*, no. 7 (1982): 12.

31. Pérez, interview not published by Ingrid Quintana-Guerrero, 2019.
32. One of the issues that clearly illustrates the editorial turn of *ARS* was the publication of the commemorative centenary of Le Corbusier's birth in 1987.
33. Pérez, interview not published by Ingrid Quintana-Guerrero, 2019.
34. Doblado, "Influencia del posmodernismo en la arquitectura de Lima 1980-2000," 49.
35. "Within postmodernism, typology was used as a mechanism to acquire a national identity, as Waisman points out, for whom the typological study requires an acute critical vision to effectively become a suitable instrument for the consolidation of a national or regional identity." Ibid., 70.
36. Ibid., 45; 50.
37. Ibid., 42.
38. Beingolea del Carpio, José. "Crisis de la arquitectura y/o arquitectura de la crisis." In *Arquitectura limeña de hoy*. Exhibition Catalogue. Lima: Editorial Arius, 1992, 30.
39. Ortiz de Zevallos, Augusto. "Abajo el funcionalismo. Y arriba, ¿qué? (I)." *El Mirador de Lima. Debate*, no. 16 (1982): 71-76.
40. Doblado, "Influencia del posmodernismo en la arquitectura de Lima 1980-2000," 40.
41. Ibid., 69.
42. Beingolea del Carpio, "Crisis de la arquitectura y/o arquitectura de la crisis," 30.
43. "The first seeks a return to architectural specificity by looking for symbols and forms that convey meanings that are easy to capture, although they may be ambiguous and left to the author's free creativity [...]. The other group, historical postmodernism [...] proposes a study of urban culture values based on the history of the city, using typological study and urban morphology as instruments." Doblado, "Influencia del posmodernismo en la arquitectura de Lima 1980-2000," 20.
44. Besides to the mentioned work, among his publications that had a great impact in the 80s are *El uso de las ciudades y de las viviendas* (1978) and *Casas y Escritos* (1989). Regarding his built work during his post-modern phase, the Consorcio Nacional de Seguros – Vida (Santiago, 1990-1991), and Tribunales (1996) stand out, both in association with Borja Huidobro.
45. García Alvarado, Rodrigo. "Esbozos de teoría de la arquitectura en Chile." *Arquitecturas del Sur* 24, no. 32 (July 2006): 62-69 <https://revistas.ubiobio.cl/index.php/AS/article/view/861>.
46. Frampton, Kenneth. "Towards a Critical Regionalism: Six Points for an Architecture of Resistance." *Perspecta: The Yale Architectural Journal*, no. 20 (1983): 147-162.

47. "This classification allows him to organize a diversity of work in different periods, although naturally in the 'development' there are mainly public buildings and in the 'other', regional domestic works, distinguished more than anything by their magnitude and constructive systems." García Alvarado, "Esbozos de teoría de la arquitectura en Chile," 66.
48. Ibid., 66.
49. Thanks to the author's fieldwork in 2019 at Faculty of Architecture, Design and Art – FADA of The Asunción Nacional University UNA (Paraguay), it was possible to verify that architecture research prior to 2000 is still scarce in that country.
50. "The cognitive process is nothing more than the possibility of conferring meaning on the things around us, and such a possibility is offered to us by the signs that are linked between our subjective consciousness and the world of phenomena. Signs are, therefore, the first characteristic instruments of all communication. One thing is certain: architecture, like all art, can and should be considered as an organic and, to some extent, institutionalized whole of signs and, as such, can be identified, at least partially, with other structures." Dorfles, Gillo. *Símbolo, comunicación y consumo*. Barcelona: Lumen, 1975.
51. Morra, César Augusto. *Espacios intermedios: un análisis de la arquitectura contemporánea paraguaya*. Asunción: Arquitrabe, 2000, 364.
52. Morra, *Espacios intermedios*, 185.
53. Ibid., 304.
54. Venturi, Robert. *Complejidad y contradicción en arquitectura*. Barcelona: Gustavo Gili, 1995.
55. One of the most celebrated work of Paraguayan postmodernity, the new headquarters of the Banco Central (1984), was the product of a contest won by a team of Argentine architects. Cf. Verri Lopes, Eduardo. "Aproximações sobre arquitetura paraguaia contemporânea." Master Thesis, Universidade Estadual de Maringá, Paraná, 2016 <http://repositorio.uem.br:8080/jspui/handle/1/3375>, 34.
56. "Theorists have delved into the urban structure, always trying to perceive the fixed points, the true structural knots of the city, those points where reason was carried out." Rossi, Aldo. La arquitectura de la ciudad. Barcelona: Gustavo Gili, 1981.
57. Morra, *Espacios intermedios*, 301.
58. The Finansud building in the residential neighborhood Villa Morra by these authors stands out: "By [...] proposing dominance over the corner, a dialogue with the street and a homogeneous reading with the natural fabric of the adjacent buildings this idea is clearly exposed [...] which considers the question of building typology as a possible and real link to the recognition of space and time. The appropriation of that

particular corner determines the precise conditions that drive formal management subject to the designer's interest in revaluing the environment's conditions but in a special way, to exalt the fundamental relationship between the project and the site, to make it a substantial part of the city, as an active element in its complex structure." Ibid., 302.
59. Verri Lopes, "Aproximações sobre arquitetura paraguaia contemporânea."
60. Especially this Argentine architect, who is called Pablo Capelletti, usually the examples of his classes are given from many of these architects who were from the Faculty of Venice, for example Aymonino, Aldo Rossi [...]. The Biennale di Venezia, with Aldo Rossi. Even the famous Venice Charter of restoration. So all this was a historic moment in which you follow a few architects of the generation mine, all had at least curiosity to pass by. Cf. Corvalán, Javier. "Un fin del mundo: fragmento de el libro negro." *Rita: revista indexada de textos académicos*, no. 1 (2014): 40-43 <http://ojs.redfundamentos.com/index.php/rita/article/view/39/30> quoted in Verri Lopes, "Aproximações sobre arquitetura paraguaia contemporânea," 36.
61. Cf. Corvalán, "Un fin del mundo."

The Eighties: Other Architectures from Medellín, Colombia
David Vélez Santamaría

> *The current generation of designers, academics, critics, clients, politicians and architecture bureaucrats in Colombia will surely not be so severely questioned for their lack of talent (perhaps some of that exists, although supremely well concealed); as for their inability and weakness to solve spatially the crucial cultural, urban and economic challenges of the great social majorities; for its fatuous and grandiloquent aesthetic-functionalist games and for producing an architecture in essence uncharacterized (ambivalent between nostalgic and internationalist) without socio-cultural commitments and falsified in multiple directions.*
> Héctor Wolff, "Inequidad y grandilocuencia"[1]

With these words, Héctor Wolff[2] presented his article "Inequidad y grandilocuencia" for the magazine *Proa*, in March 1987. The architect expressed his disapproval of the professional development of recent years which, in his words, was blatantly debated between real estate speculation and bad adaptations of foreign styles, issues that contributed little to the solution of the genuine problems in Colombian architecture.

During the eighties, most of the country's problems could be found in Colombian cities. They became the scene of political and social conflicts, determined by the economic crisis, daily violence, and drug trafficking. Certainly, these circumstances manifested on several scales within the urban space, which created a pessimistic panorama and a lack of horizon for architecture and urbanism. However, as indicated by the historian Luis Fernando González Escobar in his book *Ciudad y arquitectura urbana en Colombia*, this decade was the period in which transformation began.

> It can be said that the eighties were a decade of deep crisis, but also of transitions, of emergency phenomena, some were latent for a long time and others arose as a

response to that chaotic environment and deep hopelessness that was breathed in the country.[3]

Despite such a crisis, the architectures that emerged can be considered, in retrospect, the triggers of change. In many cases, these resulted from chance or purely commercial purposes and had no direct relationship with the formation of the city. However, as positive effects, their arrival ignited other possibilities of urban architecture.

For the Argentine critic Marina Waisman, these architectures represent the absorption of some forms of modernity and others of post-modernity – as a consequence of – "the general drive of the world,"[4] and not necessarily an answer to their own questions. With this, the direct relationships between technical, economic, and social transformations and architectural conceptualizations are more difficult to establish in Latin American works.

The task in this chapter is to expose part of the building production of Medellín (Colombia) during the eighties and its relationship with the discourses around the architecture practice and city. This contributes to what is raised in the work of some authors who addressed the issue of architecture produced during this decade – although tangentially as it is not their focused period. They begin to be considered an architecture that dialogues directly with the idea of the city.

One of these authors is Luis Fernando González Escobar, who highlighted the importance of restoration work and cultural infrastructure to aid in renovating the urban space of Medellín. In 1993, Silvia Arango also describes trends and new works in several cities in the country, at the time she published her book *Historia de la arquitectura en Colombia*. Meanwhile, in her work *Región y lugar en la arquitectura latinoamericana contemporánea* from 2000, Beatriz García Moreno highlights Latin American architects who developed projects in Medellín and the relationship between their production and others in different towns. Other authors working on this subject include Clara Inés Rodríguez and

Juan Carlos Pérgolis-Valsecchi. In their article "La reacción a la ciudad moderna en los años ochenta: una década de reflexión", they explain the influence of the new European theories published in the magazine *Escala* – at national level – and the construction of some relevant works. However, they only present one from Medellín.

Following the above and to relate the practice and discourses of the eighties in Medellín, specialized publications on the city's production during this decade were collected, both from practice and theory and criticism. The magazines *Proa* and *Re-vista del Arte y la Arquitectura en Colombia* were of great contribution, as well as pioneering books on the local "contemporary" work such as *Colombia: el despertar de la modernidad* from 1991 and *Arquitectura contemporánea en Medellín* from 2003. Both works of greater visibility and others less mediatic are presented following the contextualization of Medellín's circumstances during this decade. Although the work exhibited below begins with the preceding architectures, it does not follow a chronological order. Instead, it is organized using current topics of discussion: technique and heritage, housing explorations, and new styles.

In the first category *technique and heritage*, there are pioneering works in urban recycling or heritage conservation that were developed by architects of the technical generation, that is, trained in the modern school. The second category *housing explorations* group works that were built due to the housing policies of the moment and the accelerated densification promoted by real estate speculators. The third category, *new styles*, presents more controversial works because of their commercial nature, but that contributed to the urban space or the discussion of that time. The review of these works discusses how professional practice approaches and the critical discourses that accompanied the dissemination of some works began to transform the city.

The Eighties

In the eighties, the problems of violence and insecurity took hold in Medellín because of large changes in the urban structure. During this decade, the government offices moved to the new civic center La Alpujarra (1975-1987) and the financial center migrated to El Poblado sector, which accelerated the deterioration and abandonment of the traditional downtown. This situation worsened with the construction of the Metro system, a project that interrupted and paralyzed the city on several occasions, and the proliferation of enclosed complexes,[5] developments idealized by the real estate sector.

With these changes, the architecture of this decade reflects two tensions in the urban space. On the one hand, the privatization of public services and housing isolation, because of the fear of insecurity. On the other hand, the development of commercial projects in strategic areas to take even more advantage of the land. This production was permeated by new international fashions and consumption styles, as mentioned by Wolff (1987) according to the professional views of experienced architects and new talents in search of recognition.

Technique and Heritage

Since the seventies, the development of architecture in Medellín has been characterized by technical advances applied to ambitious projects.[6] Shopping centers were added to the new urban silhouette of skyscrapers. San Diego (built in 1972) was the first of these types of buildings in Colombia, which became a reference for city life.[7]

An alternative formulated to build projects of this type was the recycling of existing structures.[8] Almacentro[9] and Villanueva[10] (1981-1983) stood out for being part of the shopping centers that were inaugurated at the beginning of the decade, but also for being developed through recycling or restoration.

The Almacentro shopping center, designed by the architects Luz Ceballos, Laureano Forero,[11] and José Nicholls[12] was proposed under the principle of taking advantage of a set of warehouses with more than 8,000 square meters in the Perpetuo Socorro sector, which included an office tower. In the case of Villanueva – also developed by Luz Ceballos and Laureano Forero with Óscar Mesa[13] and Juan Posada[14] –, the project involved restoring the heritage building of the old Major Seminary and adding a new block as part of the new shopping center program.

The two works use a harmonious plastic language reminiscent of Aldo Rossi's Italian neo-nationalism, simple volumes that were built or finished with traditional materials such as brick. This harmonized with the existing heritage complex in Villanueva and allowed a play of rhythms in the facades of Almacentro. Both buildings are surrounded by high-traffic roads, which makes it difficult to connect with El Prado and San Diego neighborhoods, respectively. With the Villanueva commercial center, it was possible to mitigate the effects caused by the Oriental Avenue layout from the seventies, thanks to the outdoor galleries of the new wing. However, the intervention of Almacentro did not have the same success, due to its low permeability in front of the El Poblado Avenue.

Thanks to these types of work, the Forero-Ceballos couple and Óscar Mesa at Arquitectos Ltda. were the most outstanding figures of Medellín's building production between the late seventies and much of the eighties. It is also significant that the repertoire consolidated by these architects was determined by an awareness of technique, although from two opposing perspectives. While in the Forero-Ceballos couple's proposals architecture is developed with technical rigor, in the case of Mesa there is a search for monumentality with few resources.

The Forero-Ceballos couple explored various architectural languages, where diversity was as praised as it was questioned by critics of the time. As Luis Fernando Molina

Interior detail of Villanueva Shopping Centre. Source: David Vélez Santamaría, 2021.

Londoño indicated, Forero was a "very versatile and controversial professional, who, despite his long career and abundant production"[15] could not establish an identity of his own but stood out for his ingenuity to solve difficult technical problems. In several testimonies Forero has admitted his fascination with the diversity of architectural forms, although without theory: "It is much more difficult to be a follower of a theory than of a form, a form can be repeated as many times as you like, theory has to be studied in depth to be followed."[16]

He also mentioned the impact that the proposals of postmodern architects of the international scene had on his work and that of many of his colleagues at that time:

Krier made us think about the context, the architecture of the place; number of conditions that at least keep the identity alive... with post-modernity particularly in people like me, who came from the other side, there was an absolutely wonderful wake-up call.[17]

As for Mesa, his testimonies recount the pragmatism of Arquitectos Ltda. office and the need not to copy styles, "We are in a demanding decade that can only be faced with criteria. And the criteria are not obtained by chopping from here and there."[18] The work that partly synthesizes this thought is the Simón Bolívar Metropolitan Theatre, a project commissioned by the Medellín Cultural Association that was completed in 1987. The building was designed as a new example of modern technical tradition, "following utilitarian building criteria that exempt from any luxury or excess but takes into account that a work of this kind occurs rarely in the life of a city."[19]

Metropolitan Theatre.
Source: Germán Tamayo, 2021.

Mesa's references can be related to Louis Kahn's reflections, whose institutional buildings spread in the sixties and seventies, a period in which Mesa carried out his studies at the University of Washington, Seattle. Mesa's considerations of materials, civic buildings, and their presence in the city as monuments are close to Kahn's approach regarding social architecture from a structural logic, permanence, and millenary forms. In this sense, it is important to point out how during the seventies brick became popular again as one of the most used materials in construction in Medellín. Its application in buildings such as the metropolitan theater dignified and claimed this construction technique.[20]

Due to its presence, scale, and location, this theater is undoubtedly one of the most significant architectures in the city. The development of La Alpujarra II (1969-1974), today Plaza Mayor Square, began with its construction near the exhibition palace[21] and the new administrative center La Alpujarra.

Simultaneous with the recycling works, the shopping centers adaptations, and the construction of the new theater,[22] restorations of some historic buildings in the center started to affect the immediate environment. In 1985, work began to recover the Antioquia Railway old station, in 1986 the Auditorium of the University of Antioquia and San Ignacio Square, and in 1987 the Palace of Culture – former Government Office.

Complementary to the work of the Paraninfo, one of the few new projects that framed the Plazuela de San Ignacio was built. This building for the Confama's services unit San Ignacio (1987-1991) was by the architects José Nicholls and Condiseño Ltda. In a postmodern historicist language, the building is surrounded by open galleries, with segment arches and topped with a twelve-level office tower. The materials of the facade, such as granite basement rock and split block, give it a robust appearance, in accordance with neighboring heritage buildings. While this work was a singular commission for a cultural building with a library, most of the works by Condiseño Ltda. from the late seventies and much of the eighties were developed under a corporate vision. In this firm, the "systematization of design and construction"[23] were fundamental aspects to achieve in large housing projects.[24] Real estate business commissions provided a solution to housing demand but were questionable due to their isolation.

Housing Explorations

As indicated at the start of this chapter, during the eighties, the production of housing in Medellín was abundant but determined mainly by the promotion of closed complexes, offering to guarantee security amongst the violence that the city was experiencing. It is important to highlight that, during this decade, there were still benefits granted by financing bodies such as the Instituto de Crédito Territorial (Territorial Credit Institute), the Banco Central Hipotecario – BCH (Central Mortgage Bank) and savings and housing corporations working with a credit system based on a constant purchasing power units – known as UPAC.[25] While the wealthiest sectors were isolated in urbanizations that were concentrated in the south, in neighborhoods such as El Poblado and even in the surrounding municipality of Envigado, other traditional neighborhoods had an opulent development of buildings that stood out for their adequate insertion and adaptation to the neighborhood scale. It is necessary to talk about previous housing works also designed by the Forero-Ceballos couple in collaboration with Arquitectos Ltda. Works such as Urbanal de Laureles (1979-1981) and Ciudad San Diego (1981-1986) showed possibilities to develop housing projects with a different approach to the already established by city center's apartment towers or enclosed complexes.

Urbanal de Laureles (1979-1981) is perhaps the most remarkable housing project that was built at the beginning of this decade. It is a rental building comprised of a six-story block with a sinuous shape in front of the Church La Consolata (1966-1968).[26] The block is set back with a waving form to generate a square that receives the pedestrian and offers a plinth for commercial premises. The "open" ground floor, the running windows, and the habitable terrace recall principles of modern architecture or, as Forero indicated, the influence of Boston in the seventies. Regarding materiality, Forero refers to brick as a material with which "you could make very good architecture, Rogelio Salmona proved it, so we chose to work with brick, but with paisa brick,[27] which is very different from Bogotá."[28]

Another project where the site was carefully treated was the Plaza de la Iglesia (Church Square) I and II (1983-1985) by the architects Álvaro Restrepo[29] and Luis Fernando Ramírez.[30] Also located in Laureles, in a triangular site, this project is configured as an L block with galleries extending on the ground floors, which protects the pedestrian and serves as a transition between some commercial premises and the accesses to the whole complex. The rotation of the facade produces a corner chamfer marked with an opening, a popular detail in some works of the Italian architect Mario Botta.

However, the work that best dialogues with the city flow is the third stage of Nueva Villa del Aburrá (1979-1986), a

Nueva Villa del Aburrá.
Source: German Tamayo, 2021.

project led by the architect Nagui Sabet[31] in collaboration with Beatriz Estrada,[32] Jorge Mario Gómez,[33] and Jorge Janna.[34] The development of this complex resulted from a public tender called in 1979 by the BCH to "offer housing and services within the reach of a greater number of people"[35] in the Belén sector. Sabet's proposal stands out by offering a consistent urban solution, with outdoor galleries and a square of baroque reminiscence, rich in activity. Both the gallery and the square link the development with the existing villa. In this context, it is appropriate to highlight the reflections of one collaborator, Jorge Mario Gómez, who in the same year of the competition (1978) wrote for the *Re-vista del Arte y la Arquitectura en Colombia*:

> New projects that are being executed outside the city center in less established areas should consider the quality of the designed public space and the possibility of completing a healthier structure, in which citizens can carry out collective activities or at least identify these sites within a cultural system of urban values.[36]

Other massive housing works of that time that were significant for opening up and contributing to the urban space were the fourth and last sections of the project Carlos E. Restrepo with the Instituto de Crédito Territorial (1984-1987) and the five stages of the building complex La Mota (1982-1987), both in charge of the Forero-Ceballos couple. In both cases, blocks of staggered height are grouped "around perfectly defined public spaces, and with no access restrictions."[37] As for the formal aspects, the Carlos E. Restrepo is a more austere project of simple appearance without ornamentation, while in La Mota historicist elements were defined such as arched thresholds, bridges, and towers reminiscent of a medieval European city.

Safety in these complexes became more difficult over time, and additional enclosures were used to restrict the flow of visitors. In works such as El Enclave (1982), also in the La

Mota sector, the designer in charge from Arquitectos Ltda., Marco Aurelio Montes,[38] complied with the task of designing an enclosed complex, with the confidence that at some point it could be opened for the enjoyment of the citizens. Thus, "the occupation of the property aims to optimize and hierarchize the common spaces [...] taking as a reference the French architects group comprised by Candilis, Josic and Woods."[39]

It is worth mentioning the smaller-scale works that were carried out in neighborhoods such as Laureles and Manrique. In Laureles, a sector that was already consolidated urbanistically, an aggressive process of re-densification began in the seventies. However, the buildings Torre de Laureles (1981), by Arquitectos Ltda; Colinas (1980-1982), Capri (1983) and Cerros del Nogal (1983-1984), by architect Héctor Wolff, and the Monteblanco apartments (1989), by Juan Felipe Gómez,[40] were inserted strategically between other buildings of similar height and with appropriate setbacks to provide fair studio apartments or family accommodation design. From the outside, Torre de Laureles and the Monteblanco apartments are simple volumes, with exposed brick finish and some fine concrete details. Wolff's proposals are more controversial. They were developed as alternatives to housing typologies and make up an interesting piece in the urban landscape by including balconies, railings, and lintels that tend to contrast with their decorative characteristics.

In the Manrique neighborhood, in the city's northeast, the architects Santiago Caicedo and Patricia Gómez[41] also developed a smaller-scale work. According to their own description, the Manrique's small apartment building (1983) should become a brand as the theaters or cultural houses that bordered Carrera 45.[42] Besides generating a porch on the ground floors to compensate for the narrow section of the platform, the facade elements of this project are presented as additions or decorations, referring to the ambiguous formal explorations between "whites and grays," typical of the American postmodern debate.[43]

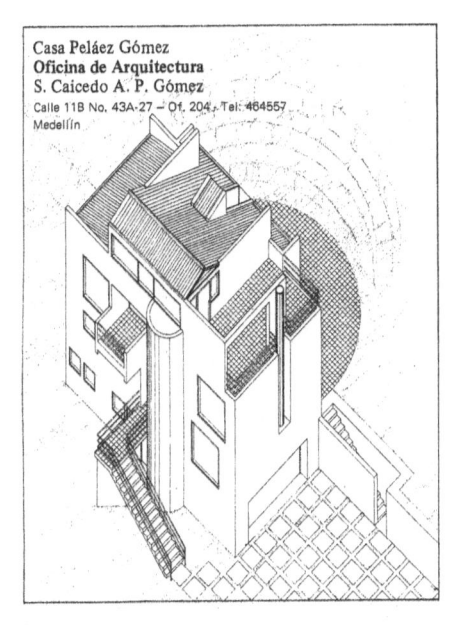

Casa Peláez Gómez
Oficina de Arquitectura
S. Caicedo A. P. Gómez
Calle 11B No. 43A-27 – Of. 204, Tel: 464557
Medellín

Advertisement from the Caicedo Gómez studio. Source: *Re-vista del Arte y la Arquitectura en Colombia*, 1978.

New Styles

Since the seventies, Caicedo and Gómez had been producing single-family housing from a critical approach. In 1978, Caicedo wrote for the *Re-vista del Arte y la Arquitectura en Colombia*, about his interest in the "whites and grays" architects of the international scene who were influencing Colombia, especially with a work of Jorge Piñol in Bogotá. This building "could be considered only (but not least) as one of the most finished and refined style exercises ever made in Colombia."[44] This allowed them to refresh the architectural debate of the moment in Bogotá, which was concentrated on rational versus organicist architecture.

The influences of American criticism were notable in the work of Caicedo and Gómez. In their retrospective monograph for *Proa* published in 1987, they referred to Michael Graves and Ricardo Bofill as examples of reflective practice and noted that "the development of the tradition of the modern is much more interesting than the careless copying of the forms of history."[45] They declared themselves postmodern modernists, which allowed us to learn from history and openly work on references, including that of Le Corbusier. According to the architects, their residence La Gavilana (1979-1981), was based on the reinterpretation of Le Corbusier's elements such as dimensions, longitudinal windows, and inverted roofs, in reference to the forest landscape on the outskirts of Medellín.

Another work in which North American influence is more evident, in this case by Venturi and Scott Brown, is the Corpavi commercial building (1984-1985), a project by Gabriel Arango,[46] Gabriel Gutiérrez,[47] and Javier Londoño, from Arquitectos e Ingenieros Asociados – AIA. This was a three-story brick volume that hosted the building program and featured elements from the Corpavi brand, in addition to a pergola supported by metal arches that completed the facade. The architects intended to create a decorated shed, a new urban symbol that would not compete with the existing ones, on a road of great commercial importance in the city center.[48]

Buildings for new medium-scale commercial headquarters, such as Corpavi, were commonly commissioned by the middle of the decade, especially toward the new center consolidating in El Poblado. Among these projects was the building for the headquarters of Banco Comercial Antioqueño and Conavi (1986) by Óscar Mesa with Arquitectos Ltda. In this building on El Poblado Avenue, similar strategies to those applied in the Metropolitan Theatre were used, such as brick towers, square blocks, and the spatial meshes that sheltered a pedestrian access atrium.

In 1980, Arquitectos Ltda. also designed one of the first corporate headquarters on El Poblado Avenue. The El Corfin Center, built as a block on a narrow site, uses exceptional language compared to the rest of the studio's work. The towers that comprised the spaces such as the vertical circulation were finished in textured concrete blocks. These served as a structure to support the large spanning volumes that sheltered the office spaces and freed the first floors, allowing fluid pedestrian access.

Another work that was a pioneer in the landscape's colonization of El Poblado Avenue is the Santillana Centre (1980-1982) by the architect Augusto González.[49] This office complex resulted from a competition promoted by the Santillana Group for an administrative headquarters. This was corporate architecture, with glassed blocks and pronounced corners, such as those of the Vicente Uribe Rendón building (1977-1980). It was surrounded by open galleries that limited a semi-public pedestrian street, directly connected to the two artery roads that surround the property.

Santillana Complex perspective 1984. Source: Free use image from Departamento Administrativo de Planeación de Medellín.

The small gestures of El Corfin center and the Santillana complex, such as the first permeable floors or the open inner street, over time, contributed to many of the new projects that limited the El Poblado Avenue. They considered these types of strategies to provide quality pedestrian space, although these transitional building spaces do not configure the public space in a strict sense.

The only space that was representative and public in the sector was the El Poblado Park, hosting the Church of San José (1904-1923).[50] In 1985, in this park – originally a square –, Laureano Forero and José Nicholls proposed an ambitious project to pedestrianize the surrounding streets and build mixed-use buildings. In the description of this proposal, both architects advocate for an architecture of collective relevance:

> With the same criteria with which the official entity obliges citizens to provide areas that will be destined for public use, we have considered that it is also possible to be forced to build facades of public enjoyment, which allows to give fair and dignified ordering to those walls that serve as a limit to the spaces of community use.[51]

Unfortunately, only two of the five buildings could be built from this project: the Aliadas Centre (1985-1987)[52] to the south side, which was intended to be a shopping center, housing Poblado Plaza (1994), an office block. In both, brick was again used as a neutral material, which allowed dialogue with the existing Church and galleries that serve to protect the pedestrian. In Aliadas, a semi-circular arch with Tuscan columns was also included, as an element to highlight the Church.

Conclusions

The set of projects discussed here is useful to approach a panorama of architectural production in Medellín in such a period of controversy and change as the eighties. As initially mentioned, there was not a common project for the architecture that emerged then, amid a disorientation in the vision of the city. The works were mostly isolated episodes, driven by some cultural initiatives, the professional aims of the authors, and above all, by commercial dynamics.

Regarding technical aspects and heritage, the architects included here have been designated by contemporary critics as heirs of the modern project or as the sons of the modern tradition.[53] Mesa and the Forero-Ceballos couple were trained abroad, with emphasis on technology, in modern schools immersed in some of the late modernity discourses or the first postmodern theories. The first works carried out by these architects at the beginning of the decade – shopping centers focusing on scale and constructive quality – can be considered as the starting point for heritage recovery and predecessors of other works that had a greater impact, such as the Metropolitan Theatre.

It is from the conception of housing that the most effective or critical discourses can be tackled, according or not to postmodern theories. Nagui Sabet, Jorge Mario Gómez, Héctor Wolff, Santiago Caicedo, and Patricia Gómez were architects also trained abroad who were aware of the new theories about architecture and the city, which influenced their housing proposals, as noted about the Nueva Villa del Aburrá and some intermediate scale buildings. Faced with the crisis regarding the functional vision of the city, and the contradictory policies for land occupation and mass housing production, their proposals were directly influenced by the international scene during the formative years. The idea of making a city, inspired by León Krier or Archigram's ideas from the Architectural Association, was a positive novelty for the urban space.

As for the styles, it should be clarified that it was by the end of the decade that the absorption of international fashions occurred with a greater force. If there is something that characterized the eighties, it was the bombardment of consumer images, and fashion facades taken as a reference in the academia and professional practice. The contaminated works are evidence of the fascination with freedom of expression that could manifest in architecture through some styles, especially in buildings of commercial use such as Corpavi by AIA, or the late explorations of the Forero-Ceballos couple. Other buildings are based on the regressive formulas of previous productions, such as Óscar Mesa's projects in Arquitectos Ltda. or Augusto González.

Finally, it should be noted that the eighties' production marks a key moment in the architecture of the city. In the first instance, it is the period in which an attempt is made to find a theory that puts architecture in context with the city, with which the explorations of architects are subsequently justified. Even when most late cases can be defined as style exercises, there is at least a stance on how architecture serves the city.

Secondly, although these projects were primarily commercial commissions, they achieved contributions in the urban space: they were urban architectures. The question of the correct appearance or shapes of these buildings takes a back seat, as it manages to establish new relationships with the street and the scale of the pedestrian. Their heterogeneity, from Waisman's approach, was positive, as they put themselves in context with the city, which marked the beginning of a new transformation of Medellín.

This moment is significant for the gestation of another architectural purpose in the city, from the new generations in the architecture faculties and their intellectual restlessness in recognizing city values. With the dispersed construction of these individual projects (but collective contributions) and an atmosphere of discussion around new theories, the eighties prepared Medellín for a new era of great public space projects, urban planning, and strategic ideas of the so-called social urbanism.

Notes

1. Wolff, Héctor. "Inequidad y grandilocuencia." *Proa* 1, no. 358 (1987): 36-39.
2. Héctor Jaime Wolff Isaza (b. 1946) was an architect from the National University of Colombia, Medellín. He had postgraduate studies from the University of London (England) and worked as teacher and dean of the Faculty of Architecture.
3. González Escobar, Luis Fernando. *Ciudad y arquitectura urbana en Colombia, 1980-2017*. Medellín: Universidad de Antioquia, 2020, XV.
4. Waisman, Marina. "Para una caracterización de la arquitectura latinoamericana." *Arquitecturas del Sur* 5, no. 14 (1989): 8-10.
5. As indicated by Arango Escobar, Gilberto, Pedro Pablo Peláez Bedoya, and Gilda María Wolf Amaya. *La poética de la vivienda*. Medellín: Editorial Universidad Nacional de Colombia, 2013, 125. Urban planning regulations in El Poblado neighbourhood were changed from the Sixties. This is a socioeconomic affluent sector in the south of the city in which, until that moment, housing development were restricted to single-family homes. New legislation allowed multifamily developments under the modality of complexes. This change followed the recommendations of a study by the real estate sector and construction companies in the city, commissioned by the Municipality's Planning Office.
6. The great verticalization of Medellín's center happened in this decade, including the Coltejer building (1972), the Torre del Café (1975), the Cámara de Comercio (1974) and the Torre Colseguros (1980).
7. Between 1978 and 1986 alone, six other shopping centers were built in Medellín, not counting predecessors such as downtown passages and chain department stores. The first shopping centers were Oviedo (1979), Camino Real (1980), Almacentro (1982), Villanueva (1982), Monterrey (1985) and Galerías de San Diego (1986). The paradigm of shopping centers in Colombian cities and their urban effects is addressed by historian Luis Fernando González Escobar, *Ciudad y arquitectura urbana en Colombia, 1980-2017*, 88.
8. In a publication in 1979 in the magazine *Proa* there was a proposal for a shopping center with the name of Capicentro in the old factory Triconova, located in the Caribe sector of the city. This project was not built.
9. National Architecture Award of the Colombian Architects Society – SCA in 1983.

10. Honorable Mention Quito Architecture Biennial 1986.
11. Laureano Forero (b. 1937) and Luz Elena Ceballos (b. 1940) are two Architects from the National University of Colombia, Medellin. Forero has postgraduate studies from The Architectural Association and married Ceballos. Both founded the architecture studio L. H. Forero in Medellin
12. José Nicholls Posada (b. 1946) is an architect from the National University of Colombia, Medellín and cofounder of the design and construction company Condiseño.
13. Óscar Mesa (b. 1945) is an architect with a masters from the University of Washington and founder of the studio Arquitectos Ltda.
14. Juan José Posada Gutiérrez is an architect from the Pontifical Bolivarian University – UPB and cofounder of the design and construction firm Convel S. A.
15. Molina Londoño, Luis Fernando. "Arquitectura del Valle de Aburrá." In *Historia de Medellín*, vol. 2, edited by Jorge Orlando Melo González, 622-641. Medellín: Suramericana de Seguros, 1966, 637.
16. Laureano Forero, interview not published by David Vélez Santamaría, 2013.
17. Ibid.
18. Mesa, Óscar. *Óscar Mesa arquitectura y ciudad*. Mexico City: Menhir Libros, 1997, 26.
19. Ibid, 26.
20. In addition to the works already described, the Forero-Ceballos couple independently developed some smaller-scale buildings in which brick is the protagonist, such as the basic care center of San Benito (1980), which was discreetly inserted into a mixed-use block in the traditional center. See Forero, Laureano, and Beatriz García Moreno. *Forero: 50 años de arquitectura*. Medellín: Laureano Forero y Compañía, 2011.
21. Work of Rodrigo Arboleda.
22. Another representative work in which Óscar Mesa participated was the outdoors "Carlos Vieco" theater (1984) in the Cerro Nutibara, part of the project to convert this hill in a park public.
23. Condiseño Ltda., and L. H. Forero Arquitectura. "Centro comercial 'Almacentro'. Medellín, 1980." *Proa* 1, no. 316 (1983): 48-53.
24. Altos de Calasanz and Altos del Rodeo were some big housing projects of enclosed complexes built in that decade by Design Ltda. with Conconcreto S. A. and Con-restructura Ltda.
25. From this moment forward, speculation was encouraged in the construction of collective housing in the country. Consequently, the BCH had a period of great constructive boom with complex projects that covered large urban sectors.

26. Work of the architects Apolinar Restrepo and Elías Zapata.
27. According to Forero, the traditional Bogotá brick has English dimensions, while the paisa brick used in Medellín was 10x20x40cm. Unlike the Bogotá brick, which can be manipulated with one hand by a builder, the paisa brick requires both hands. See Téllez Mosquera, Fernando. "Lirismo material. Expresividad técnica en la arquitectura de Laureano Forero." PhD diss., Escuela de Arquitectura, 2016 <https://repositorio.unal.edu.co/handle/unal/59705>, 203.
28. Ibid., 203.
29. Alvaro Restrepo Patiño is an architect from the UPB.
30. Luis Fernando Ramírez Franco (b. 1960) is an architect from the UPB.
31. Nagui Sabet is an architect from the University Degli Studi Di Roma and Harvard University, Graduate School of Design. He founded the studio Nagui Sabet Architecture that has branches in Medellín, Bogotá and Cali.
32. Beatriz Estrada de Nova is an architect graduated from the National University of Colombia Bogotá. She developed several projects in the landscape line and was president of the Colombian Society of Architects between 2003 and 2005.
33. Jorge Mario Gómez (b. 1950) is an architect from the UPB with a master's in arts from the Royal College of Arts. He has been a professor at the National University of Colombia Medellin, as well as dean of the same Faculty.
34. Jorge Ramón Janna David is an architect from the UPB. He is a renowned plastic artist and art restorer.
35. Condiseño Ltda., and L. H. Forero Arquitectura, "Centro comercial 'Almacentro'. Medellín, 1980."
36. Gómez, Jorge Mario. "Propuesta para la definición de un espacio público en la manzana de la gobernación de Antioquia." *Re-vista del Arte y la Arquitectura en Colombia* 1, no. 2 (1978): 10-13, 10.
37. Condiseño Ltda., and L. H. Forero Arquitectura, "Centro comercial 'Almacentro'. Medellín, 1980."
38. Marco Aurelio Montes (b. 1944) is an architect from the UPB. In addition to working with Arquitectos Ltda. he has been an outstanding professor at the National University of Colombia.
39. Chávez Giraldo, Juan David, and Marco Aurelio Montes Botero. *Obra 6. Seis lecciones de arquitectura en la producción de Marco Aurelio Montes Botero.* Medellín: La Carreta, 2019, 229.
40. Juan Felipe Gómez Tobón (b. 1945) is an architect from the UPB, a photographer and a teacher.

41. Santiago Caicedo Rico (b. 1946) is an architect from the UPB. Ana Patricia Gómez (b. 1950) graduated from the Architectural Association in London and completed a master's degree in Geography from the Agustín Codazzi Institute. In addition to her teaching and design work, she helped founding the Museum of Modern Art of Medellín – MAMM.
42. Arquitectos e Ingenieros Asociados – AIA. "Edificio 'Corpavi'. Medellín AIA." *Proa*, no. 358 (1987): 26-29.
43. While the "whites" assume that architectural forms can be reduced to an ahistorical zero-degree through structure, the "grays" aimed for the persuasion of the assembly and the relocation of architectural memory. The group of "whites" includes four of the New York Five: Peter Eisenman, John Hejduk, Richard Meier y Charles Gwathmey. In the group of the "grays" were Charles Moore, Robert Venturi and Denise Scott Brown. Michael Graves was at an intermediate point in the discussion.
44. Caicedo, Santiago. "Un paréntesis blanco en la arquitectura colombiana." *Re-vista del Arte y la Arquitectura en Colombia* 1, no. 2 (1978): 42-45.
45. Pérez Jaramillo, Jorge. "Conversación con Santiago Caicedo y Patricia Gómez". *Proa* 1, no. 366 (1987): 10-22, 10.
46. Gabriel Jaime Arango Villegas (b. 1958) is an architect from the UPB. Co-founder of Arquitectos Ingenieros Asociados S. A.
47. Gabriel Gutiérrez (b. 1959) is an architect from the Pontifical Bolivarian University, who practices performing arts and teaching.
48. Vélez White, Mercedes Lucía. *Arquitectura contemporánea en Medellín*. Medellín: ITM, 2003, 118.
49. Augusto González Velázquez (b. 1929 - d. 2011) was an architect from the Pontifical Bolivarian University and professor and dean at the same institution. In addition to the Vicente Uribe Rendón building, he designed the José María Córdova airport in Rionegro.
50. Project by Horacio Marino Rodríguez and Agustín Goovaerts.
51. AIA, "Edificio 'Corpavi'. Medellín AIA."

52. Quito Architecture Biennial Award – Category Architectural Design 1986.
53. As proposed by the researchers studying the Modern Project, in the Architecture and Urban Planning Studies group at the National University of Colombia in Medellín. Read more in Cristina Vélez Ortiz et al., *Arquitectura Moderna en Medellín 1947-1970*.

New Again: Contemporary Dialogues with Architectural Modernity in Latin America
Ivo Giroto

Quero ser velho de novo eterno, quero ser novo de novo
Caetano Veloso and Gilberto Gil, "Cinema Novo"[1]

It is almost consensual, among the most prominent Latin American critics and historians, that the central characteristics of contemporary architecture in Latin America have been established since the last decade of the twentieth century. Another common observation is that among the defining features of current production, a strong relationship with the design repertoire by modern generations can be identified, both in Latin American countries and from the North-Atlantic area. Ruth Verde Zein from Brazil states:

> Various trends and contributions born from manifestations of modern architecture remain as living heritage, which continues to help the construction of contemporary Brazilian architecture. This statement seems to be confirmed, even in the second decade of this century. It also might be valid elsewhere. In much of Latin America and other parts of the world, the modern tradition has been renewed, based on the revisions brought by historical modernism. Its contributions have been recognized not only within a specific moment in the past, but also as a living, present, contradictory, and complex tradition.[2]

In the same sense, many authors consider that the twenty-first century has begun *de facto* (in fact) in the last decade of the twentieth century, not only in the specific field of architecture. Luís Fernández Galiano[3] points out that the years after the fall of the Berlin Wall dismantled the bipolar geopolitical structure, accelerated globalization, and ultimately introduced digital logic in all areas of life and human production. The idea of a globalized and supposedly borderless world assumes the emergence of an integrated planet, where monolithic national identities no longer have a place and give way to the emergence of multiple identities.

It is also necessary to highlight the profound socio-economic transformations that, throughout this period, significantly weakened the action of the National States in favor of the adoption of neoliberal policies. In Latin America, although the end-of-century context presented specific problems in each country or region, it had in common the challenge of overcoming a succession of economic, social, and political difficulties, which defined the 1980s as "the lost decade" from Mexico to Argentina. Most governments that were former promoters of major projects, since then, have given the role of privileged architecture promoter to private initiatives, which have structurally changed the scope of the architectural profession.

When considering the steep increase of architects acting in this region, the picture becomes even more complex. Unlike the mid-twentieth-century generations who graduated with a generally convergent discourse, spread throughout a few universities in each country, the "postmodern generation" that began in the mid-1970s opened a period of criticism followed by a nostalgic review of the previous generations.[4]

Indeed, between the 1980s and 1990s a process of a profound revision of the modern Latin American avant-garde work was undertaken, amid the transition between modern and postmodern, through debates, architectural exchanges, and new research within first architecture and urbanism postgraduate courses in the region.[5]

It is also usually agreed that the current architectural production, not only here, is marked by diversity, plurality, and complexity. This would reflect the postmodern condition, supposedly contrary to the totalizing and homogenizing tendency of the modern world. However, at least in the field of architecture, modern Latin American experiences are proof that there has never been "one" modern architecture, but many, and they are already diverse and plural. Likewise, from the positioning of the first modern generations and their decline in the last quarter of the twentieth century, there were intense dialectical movements between transformations and permanence, ruptures, and continuities, which refute any monolithic reading of this production.

In the study of modernity retaking as a referential source, the role played by the different twentieth-century architectural expressions regarding infrastructure construction and the countries' modern image cannot be excluded. As described by Eric Hobsbawm and Terence Ranger, the central partaking in "the invention of tradition" from many Latin American countries, gives modern architecture a different historical weight compared to the verified in Europe.[6]

The conditions to take part in the globalized world also make up a very unusual situation, one full of contrasts, which questions the complete overcoming of modernity among us. In 1990, Marina Waisman highlighted this question, stating: while the rich countries were "back from modernity," Latin America "continued on its way to it."[7] In her theoretical work, Waisman pointed out that stylistic changes did not provide reliable guidelines for the periodization of architecture on the subcontinent but gave the data governing its production and the prevailing ideologies.[8]

It may not make much sense in countries that have never completed the cycle of industrialization to speak of proper post-industrial order. Anyway, in the superposition of current times and discourses, marked by deep geopolitical, economic, and cultural asymmetries, the appropriations of modern experiences in contemporary Latin American architecture are equally dissimilar, varied, and divergent.

What is generalizable is the appropriation of modernity as a past that is still alive today. It is the center of production that takes it up and transforms it – even when it tries to overcome it – and from which should build the new. The conception of innovation that emphasizes on the past has been the heart of the modern project developed in Latin America. In countries like Brazil and Mexico, the synthesis between modernity and tradition even seemed to be expressed through an oxymoron, in which the new evoked the eternal.

Between 1990 and 2020, democratic order was imposed after decades of dictatorial regimes that devastated major countries, and relative political and economic stability was placed in much of the region's countries. Because of a brief cycle of economic prosperity, new and important public and private projects were built throughout this period, largely in the context of city marketing that defines a scenario of competition between global cities.

In this period, which is now definitively closed, modern masters had a leading presence in contemporary production, sharing the scene with later generations of architects, once again challenging recurring historiographic limits. The past decades consolidated the rescue of the modern design repertoire as the primary source of contemporary architecture, and from different approaches, it has been possible to turn it into "new again".

Narrowing the approach helps to avoid excessive schematism, common in panoramic texts. It alerts us to the risk of giving extrinsic reasoning to contemporary architects. Looking collectively at different dialogues – necessarily incomplete – that are contemporary to the modern heritage, can help to understand the sense and meanings that this "architectural future of the recent past" can still have in the present.

Previous Dialogues

Since the last decades of the last century, historiography has striven to overcome the preference for exceptional characters, atypical events, and original works in favor of a reading that demonstrates the complexity and variety that marked modern production. In this context, emphasizing well-known and studied names and trajectories may sound extemporaneous. However, the active presence of some extraordinary personalities from modern generations in the contemporary scenario of various Latin American countries cannot be ignored. Nor is the formative potential that they eventually exerted, directly or through their projects, on later generations of architects.

To investigate the role played by those who, meritoriously, are called modern "masters" in the past decades is to analyze a recently completed cycle, marked by the disappearance of what Hugo Segawa called "the remnants of an era."[9] In 1982, the death of the outstanding Mexican architects José Villagrán García and Juan O'Gorman opened a four-decade period in which all the main masters of Latin American modernity left. This is symbolically close with the death of the Brazilian Paulo Mendes da Rocha, in May 2021, exactly two years after the death of the Colombian Germán Samper Gnecco.

Belonging to two successive generations, which Silvia Arango calls *progressive* (1945-1960) and *technical* (1965-1975), these are architects mostly born between the first years of the last century and 1930.[10] Because of the experience and recognition achieved throughout their important careers, many were responsible for the most significant contemporary architecture commissions in their countries.

For example, Pedro Ramírez Vázquez (1919-2013), was the author of many of the largest Mexican museums, alongside extensive production of exceptional buildings, throughout his professional life. He belonged to the generation that added to the modern project the monumentality and plastic heritage manipulation from his country's rich pre-Hispanic history. According to Enrique de Anda, his death meant the symbolic framework of closure of the Mexican architectural-culture modernization.[11]

Without abandoning the monumental and sculptural character of the modern syntax forms – which characterize works such as the Mexican Pavilion at the International and Universal Exhibition of Brussels (1958) or the monumental National Museum of Anthropology (1963-1964) – the architect was adding to his end-of-century works aspects associated with postmodern language. This with the adoption of a strong figurative and communicative accent – as in the Cultural Centre of Tijuana (1982), the Mexican Pavilion at the Universal Exhibition of Seville (1992), or the Theatre Piedras Negras (2011).[12]

Something similar can be observed in the work of another Mexican representative, Teodoro González de León (1926-2016). His first works reflected the doctrine of Le Corbusier (1887-1965), for whom he worked in 1948. With passing time, he added pre-Hispanic volumetric references to the functionalist precepts. In the 1970s, he reached a period of maturity that culminated with works of great importance, such as the Rufino Tamayo Museum – designed in collaboration with Abraham Zabludovsky (1981). In the following decade, there was a stage in which he responded to the historicism call by adding direct references to the most notable episodes of Mexican architecture: the pre-Hispanic and colonial baroque.[13] The openness to experiment with

University Museum of Contemporary Art – MUAC (Mexico City), work by Teodoro González de León, designed in 2004 and inaugurated in 2008 to integrate the UNAM Cultural Center. Source: Ivo Giroto, 2020.

compositional and formal solutions defines what Gustavo López Padilla described as a work marked by the "constancy of change."[14]

Receptivity to the changes, which characterized the trajectories of architects such as Ramírez Vázquez and González de León, is identifiable in the works of many modern-trained architects throughout Latin America, especially among those who practiced in the second half of the last century.

An illustrative case of a turn towards the so-called postmodern was the work of the Italic-Argentine Clorindo Testa (1923-2013). In the 1980s, Testa left behind a mature repertoire of brutalist references, celebrated in projects such as the monumental National Library (1962-1992), and experimented with a metaphorical and scenographic language, visible in projects such as the Recoleta Cultural Centre (1979-1984), or the Legislative Library (2004-2006), in Santa Rosa. In this period, his projects established an intense dialogue with his paintings, as if in each new project he tried to create one of his paintings in three dimensions.

Different experiences were presented by the two most internationally recognized Brazilian architects, Oscar Niemeyer (1907-2012) and Paulo Mendes da Rocha (1928-2021). Since the end of the last century, in the subsiding of postmodern experiences, both went through a process of revaluation of their work.[15] In both cases, the permanence far exceeds the transformations identifiable throughout their trajectories. Indeed, it is easier to recognize certain exhaustion of the use of forms and strategies in many of their contemporary works than to point out changes.

In Niemeyer's work, a line of continuity can be identified from the repetition of types or formal families, arranged, and combined in different ways. Two of his most important projects in this period, the Niterói Contemporary Art Museum (1996) and the Oscar Niemeyer Museum, in Curitiba (2002), are characterized by a sculptural volume suspended on a single structural support, which finds their conceptual genesis in the non-built project for the Museum of Modern Art in Caracas, Venezuela (1954). It is just one example of the architect's recurrent use of formal families – such as the domes, shells, and vaults – developed over his seven decades of work.

Largely because of his national and international devotion, since he returned to Brazil in 1983 – after his exile in France – Niemeyer predominantly projected exceptional works with rather generic programs, such as cultural centers and exhibition spaces.[16]

The construction of the Brazilian Museum of Sculpture and Ecology – MuBE (1986-1995), in São Paulo, considered one of Mendes da Rocha's masterpieces, marked the beginning of a new cycle of prominent work. In the following three decades, the changes in the architect's way of doing and thinking were remarkable. Since his award-winning project to restructure the historic building of the Pinacoteca do Estado de São Paulo (1993-1997), his well-known exploration of raw and imperfect concrete competes with the introduction of metal structures, which lightness and precision inaugurate a new materiality order, reaching the apex with the roof for the Patriarca Square (2002) in the center of São Paulo. The work for the Pinacoteca also marks the moment in which Mendes da Rocha begins to work in partnership with younger architects' studios, establishing a less direct relationship with the drawing, now digitally drawn by the associated offices.

Between transformations and permanence, it should be noted that he never abandoned his conviction that architecture must result from the exaltation and expression of technique – a modern idea. There were no noticeable structural changes in his rigorous personal style, although, in recent works such as Lisbon's Museu Nacional dos Coches (National Coach Museum, 2008-2016) and the Cais das Artes (Quay of Arts, 2009, under construction) in Vitória, some of his past elegance was lost.

Museu Nacional dos Coches (National Coach Museum, Lisbon), designed by Paulo Mendes da Rocha in collaboration with the São Paulo office MMBB and the Portuguese architect Ricardo Bak Gordon. Source: Ivo Giroto, 2018.

The last stage of work in an artist's trajectory is usually considered a minor period, contrary to what Ezra Pound defines as the time of tender and irrepressible youth that characterizes classical work, ensured by the maintenance of an efficient, precise, and clear language.[17] Although much of the strength faded in the "late" period, the work produced by Latin American masters over the past four decades is large enough in commissions' numbers and importance to be ignored.

Formerly a support for the consolidation of national identities, the symbols produced by the masters managed to produce incomparable collective meaning. However, in many cases, the formal expressiveness that helped forge the image of modern Latin America was perfectly suited to the communicative demands of postmodern architecture. Regarding Niemeyer's work, Fernando Díez mentioned:

> He has perceived like no one else the sign of the new era, and it can be said that he was the one who managed to convert architecture to the mass communication system, anticipating for several decades the end-of-the-century phenomenon of globalization with Thomas Krens and Frank Gehry's Guggenheim Museum Bilbao.[18]

Another fundamental question is to inquire about the inheritance that they eventually passed on to later generations. Enrique de Anda[19] highlights those Mexican teachers who opened new paths and created training spaces for many followers who then proposed their visions and pointed out that their absence has meant total changes in the paradigms of production in their country.

The case of Luis Ramiro Barragán (1902-1988) is perhaps the most eloquent example of the development of a school where diffusion transcends Latin American borders. His proposal of "emotional architecture", little aligned with the ideas of the heroic Mexican architecture of the 1950s, instituted a reference that until today is used intensively. On the one hand, his work inspired the important work of architects such as Ricardo Legorreta (1931-2011), who knew how to transfer the intimate atmosphere of the master's architecture to buildings with large forms and spaces. On the other hand, his work has been manipulated to the point of boredom by hundreds of followers, who take it as a reference superficially from the reproduction of its consecrated images and compositional forms.[20]

Although Barragán shared – with his Brazilian contemporary Niemeyer – a production with a strong personal accent, the work of the latter never came to define an easily manageable architectural system as with the Mexican. Indeed, attempts to reproduce the strategies and forms of the Carioca architect can only result in caricatures of very questionable appearance. Something very different is recognized with Mendes da Rocha, which has been a primary reference for many young Brazilian architects, not only in São Paulo. Hand in hand with new generations, the design heritage of the so-called "Paulista School" – with João Batista Vilanova Artigas (1915-1985) as its first intellectual father – continues to be appropriate and reinterpreted.

Indeed, in Brazil, the reverence for the local modern tradition has not disappeared even during the postmodern boom. This will have to do with the persistence of thought and language in the work of masters, such as Niemeyer and Mendes da Rocha. It may also be related to the sociological condition of a country where the border between the modern and the postmodern has always been blurred.

For example, Niemeyer's work challenged – from the beginning – the assumptions of an architecture presented as international and falsely unrooted. The ambiguous play that characterizes his architecture – international and local, abstract, and figurative, rational and illogical, minimal and excessive – led s*ir* Nikolaus Pevsner, even in 1961, to consider that it degenerated into a "postmodern anti-rationalism," which Segawa identifies as one of the first uses of the term recorded in architectural criticism.[21]

Pevsner's pioneering remark foresaw by two decades the generalization that, from the 1980s onwards, defined as postmodern, almost everything that did not fit into the patterns identified with the established Modern-European architectural language. This is how readings based on foreign visual taxonomies faced difficulties in classifying the work of architects with solid modern training, such as Barragán, the Colombian Rogelio Salmona (1929-2007), the Italian-Brazilian Lina Bo Bardi (1914-1992), or the Brazilian Severiano Mario Porto (1930-2020).

To some extent, the heated debates about "critical regionalisms" – defiant[22] or divergent,[23] "appropriate modernity"[24] and "other architectures"[25] – which marked the last two decades of the last century, tried to solve the Latin American architectural paradox.

So, we are still "condemned to the modern?" – as the Brazilian critic Mario Pedrosa predicted in the 1950s. A possible answer was formulated by Carlos Antônio Leite Brandão when analyzing the Brazilian case, although extendable to an entire subcontinent made up of crosses and overlaps:

> Our modernism, when not bureaucratized, was something heterodox, already postmodern, and still eclectic [...] Modern and postmodern are not, in our view, successive styles in time, but forces and categories that are still in tension and work together and simultaneously, within the modern (which was already postmodern), the postmodern (which was still modern) and contemporaneity. Because of this, our contemporary architecture remains marked by pluralism, by the diversity of currents, and is, paradoxically, 'modern and postmodern'.[26]

Subsequent Dialogues

To briefly comment on the different dialogues that contemporary Latin American architects establish regarding the modern experience, it is convenient to shift the focus from exceptional trajectories and authors to examples that help illustrate some common questions and varied answers from professionals who graduated mostly after the 1980s.

In Brazil, a singular case stands out as probably the most crystalline example of an architectural lineage forged in modernity and transformed into contemporaneity. As mentioned in the previous section, a cohesive collective production was instituted in São Paulo based on the project and intellectual repertoire of its modern architecture. Until recently, Paulo Mendes da Rocha has been the custodial figure of a generation of architects who had their radiating center in the Faculty of Architecture and Urbanism at the University of São Paulo – FAU USP.

Some elements are noticeable in the works of studios such as SPBR (Angelo Bucci), Grupo SP (Alvaro Puntoni and João Sodré), MMBB (Fernando de Mello Franco, Marta Moreira and Milton Braga), and Metro Arquitetos (Martin Corullon and Gustavo Cedroni), among many others. For example, the manipulation of the defining principles of São Paulo's modernity: the containment of the program in a single volume, the expressive and material rigor, the strong technical accent, the structural rationality, and the non-obstructive space. According to the analysis of Guilherme Wisnik, this comprises a panoramic framework that allows the identification of a more "operational" than "linguistic" action.[27]

More operative, because it is based on project strategies corresponding to a specific intellectual content, which reaffirms the need to think of architecture as an urban infrastructure in a country whose socio-economic reality impels austerity. Within a culture traditionally cautious regarding form, a path of autonomy was created in the face of a "formal" international approach, which puts art before practice. For Ana Vaz Milheiro, this autonomous perspective shows the vitality of a rooted culture; a foundational brand of this Brazilian contemporaneity "that could only be installed taking into account what existed before."[28]

In historiography, the initial point for this contemporaneity is usually the project for the non-built Brazil pavilion at the Universal Exhibition of Seville in 1992, designed by Angelo Bucci, Alvaro Puntoni, and José Oswaldo Vilela. The project, which represented a turning point in the practice and criticism of Brazilian architecture, made explicit reference to the legacy of São Paulo modernity and its unfailing suspended concrete boxes, rescuing as tribute, its technical, aesthetic, and ethical dimensions.

In this same exhibition, the Chilean pavilion has also been considered as the initial framework of a new architectural culture for a country that re-opened to the world wanting to leave behind one of the most terrible civil-military dictatorships of the continent.

José Cruz Ovalle and Germán del Sol's project, besides referencing the organic forms that Alvar Aalto designed for the New York World's Fair in 1939, extensively used two Chilean natural materials: par excellence, wood, and copper. The project foreseen some characteristics that would mark the subsequent country's production: the emphasis on the material dimension, from its visual and tactile attributes to its cultural content; and the conceptual and poetic foundation protected by the aesthetic modernity archive.

Other characteristics celebrated as distinctive of current Chilean production, the conception of geography as a landscape in contrast to elementary and abstract forms, are the lessons present in Chilean modernity since the 1940s and 1950s. However, as observed by Horacio Torrent, this

Casa Cien (Concepción, Chile), residence and studio of architects Mauricio Pezo and Sofía von Ellrichshausen, built between 2009 and 2011. Source: Ivo Giroto, 2019.

work-nature relationship was not formulated as a romantic or poetic pretense, but as a way of channeling modern architecture into local conditions.[29]

The minimal and contained expression that characterizes the works of architects such as Mathías Klotz, Smiljan Radic, Cristián Undurraga, Alejandro Aravena, Mauricio Pezo and Sofía von Ellrichsrausen, among others, reintroduces a formal argument that refers to the historical avant-garde of the twentieth century. It also denotes a shift from the visual to the tactile-kinesthetic and conceptual dimension that also can be related to the experiments carried out in the Ritoque Open City, in Valparaíso, since 1970.

Parallel to the pavilion in Seville, Hugo Mondragón identifies Klotz's modest house in Tongoy (1991) as responsible for launching a manifesto on which Chilean architecture built a tacit disciplinary agreement, characterized by the boxes that have dominated the panorama since the early 1990s.[30]

In this proliferation of boxes that have marked Chilean production, Pedro Ignacio Alonso (2015)[31] sees neutrality that goes beyond the cube as a zero-state of form, for a century associated with modern non-objectivity, as argued by Kazimir Malevich and El Lissitzky. He notes that this basic geometrization is accompanied by a cancellation of the architectural constructive and tectonic dimensions in favor of a "mono-material" surface accent, which eliminates the articulation between the parts and the project's technical legibility. This attitude blurs the significant relationship between the parts and results in an eminently non-tectonic architecture.

The works of many of the most important Chilean architects today show a professional rigor well adapted to market laws and in tune with the global media context.[32] This has meant the definitive entry of Chilean architecture into the market of symbolic goods, which for Torrent indicates the "distance between the forms of aesthetic viewpoints regarding the political viewpoints."[33] It would not be too much to suggest, therefore, that in Chile production has been neutral in every way.

While in Brazil the active presence of modern epigones during the turn of the century was decisive, for better and for worse. On the one hand, it enriched the modern experience of the country; on the other, it meant an additional challenge to the emancipation of young architects.[34] In Chile, the imprint of paradigmatic masters of local modernity in the current production is noticeable only diffusely, which can mean a loss of density of the modern discourse while its forms are preserved. In Argentina, the architect Rafael Iglesia (1952-2015) – from the National University of Rosario – complained about the same. According to him, contemporary architecture lacked a theory that gave it philosophical support, and nothing surpassed the exhausted model of the last century. In his opinion, this marked a fundamental difference between the modern heritage in Argentina and Brazil.

> Buenos Aires is suffering from the lack of good architects, because they lived the modern movement as an aesthetic thing, as a style, they did not even remember about ethics. In Brazil, for example, it is different, they are ideologically communist and found a relationship between ethics and aesthetics.[35]

Iglesia's work represents the search for a practice based on theoretical foundations that discuss the structural, functional, and social dimensions of architecture. His very experimental works established a strong tension with modernity from the constant subversion of the correspondence between form and function, which enriched the meaning of the structural and material components of architecture.

In the Argentine context, his experience seemed to be exceptional, overwhelmed by the strong economic crisis that marked the country's entry into the twenty-first century after decades of neoliberal policies, which negatively affected architectural production. In the increase of public commissions between 2003 and 2015, Julio Arroyo identifies a predominance of minimalist architectures that may have more to do with the technical-constructive viability and the definition of a safe system and easy replication by municipal and provincial technical offices still responsible for a large part of the state projects in the country.[36]

Evocations of the local modern repertoire are rare, such as those by architects Mario Corea, Francisco Quijano, Luis Lleonart and Silvana Codina, who used the "umbrellas" developed by Amancio Williams since the 1940s on the central axis of the Molino Fábrica Cultural (2010) in Santa Fe. The manipulation, competent but banal, of solid and precise concrete prisms is common, such as the one that characterizes the modular and cubic architecture of the Museum of Contemporary Art of Mar del Plata (2013), designed by Monoblock.

The 2005 fall issue of the Mexican magazine *Arquine* presented the work of two contemporary architects, the Chilean Mathias Klotz and the Mexican Bernardo Gómez-Pimienta under the suggestive title "Cajas modernas" (Modern Boxes). The editorial highlighted a brief differentiation made by another Argentine architect, Jorge Moscato, who considered that "for a Chilean, architecture is the

The suspended bookshelves that characterize the interior of the Vasconcelos library (Mexico City), project by Alberto Kalach / Taller de Arquitectura X.
Source: Ivo Giroto, 2020.

landscape, for a Colombian the matter and for a Mexican the form (preferably monumental)."[37]

The observation suggests that monumentality is involved in the Mexican soul, or at least in the great state works that characterized the country's expansive cycle of modernity, still strongly penetrating the work of contemporary generations. It should be considered that the supposed Mexican attraction for monumentality is not something inherent in the architectural world but is also part of the country's political culture to which architects seek to respond.

The National Centre for the Arts – CNA, a huge and cacophonous set of schools and cultural facilities (1994), is an example of the construction of large ensembles intended to mark the administration of a certain president, in this case, Carlos Salinas (1988-1994). Other latest expressions include the Vasconcelos Library (2006) by Alberto Kalach during the presidency of Vicente Fox (2000-2006).

Fernanda Canales identifies these works as the endurance of the model of outstanding achievements crowned by successive Mexican governments since Miguel Alemán (1946-1952), with the monumental University City of the National Autonomous University of Mexico – UNAM (1952).[38] However, in opposition to the optimistic urbanism that championed the public policies of the 1950s, she points out that works such as these do not go beyond "controlled islands" in a metropolis that has lost the capacity to plan in the face of uncontrolled horizontal expansion.

In the CNA coexist works by masters such as Legorreta – project's coordinator and author of the National School of Plastic Arts – and González de León – National Conservatory of Music – with works of architects that were in the process of consolidation, such as Enrique Norten – National School of Theatre.

The Vasconcelos Library evokes – with great technical assertion – the monumentality of the modern Mexican tradition, where cultural infrastructure was a symbol of modernity construction based on the idea of stability of the pre-Hispanic past.

Norten and Kalach belong to what Enrique de Anda considers "intermediate generations,"[39] who finished their training around the 1980s. Both graduated in Mexico (Iberoamerican University) and with postgraduate degrees from the United States (Cornell University), represent a diversification moment of training and approach from the American academic universe.[40] Each one rescues, in its way, images of the avant-garde and spectacular materials and pieces of high technology. However, while Kalach proposes a critical vision and a clear work discourse "more original and sculptural in the recent Mexican panorama", Norten has been characterized by a certain "techno-internationalism" that explores the expressiveness of metallic elements in a "refined modern architecture."[41]

Indeed, since the 1990s, in various parts of Latin America, architecture aims to reproduce the techno-scientific myth of the avant-garde. In Mexico, the dissemination of a type of architecture, humorously dubbed as "*Mex-Tec*", reflected the desire for technological integration and redrawing of the country's image in a globalized world. This was driven by North American Free Trade Agreement – NAFTA, a trade agreement signed with the United States and Canada in 1994.[42]

We must not forget that this kind of illusion with the technological image has no correspondence with the current situation of the civil construction industry in Latin America. The failure of industrialized construction and mass production, as proposed by the avant-garde of the 1920s, contributed to emptying matters of moral meanings and ideological content.

In this context, the replacement of the technical-constructive emphasis with "material" or "material approaches" is better understood, which Alonso identifies in recent Chilean production, for example.[43] In his opinion, with Chile, the absence of an industrial sector of construction has led architects to move away from references to "modern construction" and to approach a discourse on the poetics of the unique matter.

Alonso seems to denounce that, in his country, architects have given up in the face of reality. After all, Latin American modernity was defined by a search for cultural and technological updating, frankly incompatible with the productive reality of the countries. This did not impede many architects who proposed prototypes that could be prefabricated, or even designed complete industrialized systems, as shown by the experience of the Brazilian João Filgueiras Lima, Lelé (1932-2014).

Although the dynamics of des-industrialization, or the non-existence of industry, can be extended to most Latin American countries, in some Chile's neighboring countries, the dimension of technology as a fundamental basis of architecture has been reaffirmed. For example, in the work of many Brazilian and Paraguayan architects, the idea that architecture is "to reason with as much ingenuity as possible"[44] – as proposed by Mendes da Rocha – is updated, which shows that industrial deficiency does not automatically result in the emptying of constructive and ideological discourse.

Even when contemporary Latin American architecture has moved away from the integrally industrialized conception as an assembly, in the work of many architects, there is a wide domain of possibilities offered by industrialized products. These are often combined with natural materials and artisanal techniques, in which attention to detail has gained prominence.

Works such as the Xul Solar Museum, in Buenos Aires, by Pablo Tomás Beitia (1987-1993) anticipated an emphasis on the treatment of surfaces and joints between parts and materials, in a sophisticated approach like that of the Italian master Carlo Scarpa (1906-1978). A meticulous approach is also in the work of Isaac Broid who in projects such as the

The translucent surface of the Moreira Salles Institute (São Paulo), a project by Andrade Morettin.
Source: Ivo Giroto, 2018.

Centro de la Imagen (Mexico City, 2012) and the Cuernavaca Auditorium (2014), shifts the emphasis from the constructive to the fine articulation between materials and textures.

In the Moreira Salles Institute (São Paulo, 2017), the architects Vinícius Andrade and Marcelo Morettin, known for exploring standard pieces and light industrial materials to extract their maximum expressive power, integrate the São Paulo design tradition and meticulous treatment of the building envelope, which translucency relates interior and exterior spaces. Although ambiguous surfaces are distinctive marks of contemporary architecture, in this case, the glass envelope surrounding the museum's internal volumes refers to another precedent, the Maison de Verre (1928-1932) by Pierre Chareau, defining an overlap of layers that seems to update Semper's textile tradition.

Also in Brazil, Angelo Bucci's work brings the technical-tectonic dimension of the so-called São Paulo School to an unprecedented formal and spatial expressiveness. In his projects, the previous brutal and vulgar expressiveness of concrete becomes smooth, using an industrial framework with a refined detail design.

Here, the details play a role that transcends the ornamental beauty and act as fundamental elements; as parts that contribute to the whole. As with the work of Mies van der Rohe (1886-1969), in the design of the details lies a discourse that unifies the industrial and artisanal fields, technique, and art. It is a kind of approximation that saves the technical accent from degenerating into technicality, although sometimes flirting with preciousness. As Bucci mentions:

> It is clear that technique has many virtues, but confidence in those virtues has a limit. And that limit sometimes comes into conflict, even because of the moment in which we currently live, in the hegemonic power of the technical-scientific, to which every cultural sense is subjugated, and which threatens us with the construction of the end of the world.[45]

Indeed, the valorization of culture, from its historical and popular dimensions, has been an important guideline for contemporary architects. The sensitivity towards indigenous knowledge, respect for pre-existence, and the expansion of heritage references is a renewed way of approaching an issue previously confronted, in a different but quite successful way, by modern Latin American architecture.

For example, in countries like Mexico and Brazil, the invention of modernity excavated the past to find the deepest roots of the national constitution.[46] While Mexicans invoked their grandiose pre-Hispanic past and treated their encounter-confrontation with Spanish culture, in Brazil, Lucio Costa formulated the thesis that the roots of modern

Brazil were in a rather humble and unsightly colonial past, then praised and monumentalized.

Since then, the oxymoron tradition-modernity has resisted the way of doing and thinking architecture in Latin America, where concepts such as complexity and contradiction are far from being a postmodern novelty. In an insightful observation, the Spanish critic Rosa Olivares asks: "Why in Mexico does everything new seem to have been there forever and only the tradition seems to be increasingly original?"[47] This inquiry could refer to both the great modern Mexican works and certain recent productions, which seek to move away from colossal and spectacular architecture.

Mauricio Rocha's work, for example, seeks support in the deep interpretation of the site and culture. His architecture usually starts from pre-existing and available technology and uses an abstract language that deliberately avoids vernacular or figurative forms.

The case of Rocha represents a generation that lived in its formative stage, the mood change, which in turn put modern architecture into question. He closely accompanied the turn towards the postmodern undertaken by his father, the modern-trained architect Manuel Rocha Díaz (1936-1996), with whom he worked until his death before associating with Gabriela Carrillo. His sensitivity to local issues, and the aesthetic accuracy with which he treats them, is surely related to the work of his mother, the acclaimed photographer Graciela Iturbide (1942).

However, much of the foundations of the discreet and integrated architecture proposed by Rocha seem to come from the master Carlos Mijares (1930-2015). The contextual emphasis, the work as an experience, its transfiguration with nature, and, especially, an architecture that knows how to silence and take part in the environments are lessons written in *Tránsitos y demoras*,[48] Mijares' book repeatedly cited by Rocha.

There are exemplary attitudes of a generation that gradually moving away from the imposing symbols of modernity,

View of the central courtyard of the San Pablo Academic and Cultural Center (Oaxaca, Mexico), a project by Mauricio Rocha and Gabriela Carrillo. Source: Hugo Segawa, 2016.

based on the idea of pre-Hispanic monumentality, to deal with more immediate and less transcendental problems in search of a "Mexicanidad otra."[49] For example, the delicate insertion of works, such as the San Pablo Academic and Cultural Centre (2012), the use of traditional techniques, such as compacted earth in the School of Visual Arts (2008), both in Oaxaca, and the tectonic order that shapes the masonry space in the study of his mother in Mexico City (2017).

The tectonic and sensitive approach gives the material a cultural and anthropological sense and continues the path from the middle of the last century by masters such as Eladio Dieste (1917-2000), Togo Díaz (1927-2009), Mijares and Salmona. Paraguayan architects currently use this tradition, the work of Solano Benítez and Javier Corvalán in particular, who developed a technical-poetic expressiveness that mixes great structural audacity with artisanal methods of bricklaying.

We must remember an important relationship built since the 1990s between Paraguayan, Brazilian, and Argentine architects – parallel to the process of regional integration promoted by Mercosur in 1991 – highlighting the friendly dialogues between Solano Benítez, Angelo Bucci and Rafael Iglesia.[50] According to Javier Rodríguez Alcalá, the links with the São Paulo school were significant and helped to rebuild a blurred relationship with the modern experiences of the 1950s-1970s, remaking inter-regional and inter-generational connections.[51]

The work of an architect like Benítez illustrates the attitude of young Latin American generations, which usually

Detail of the walkway in the Faculty of Architecture, Design, and Art at the National University of Asunción, a project by Solano Benítez built in 2014. Source: Ingrid Quintana-Guerrero, 2019.

find solutions "without finesse, but of great inventiveness", using ordinary materials and transgressing technical standards.[52]

This attitude *finds* parallel and precedent in Lina Bo Bardi's way of thinking, who in 1977 argued in *Tempos de grosura* for a collective awareness in the face of the violent and rapid process of deculturation observed in Brazil, marked by an unequal and imperfect modernization. She warned about the urgent seeking of answers in the unique anthropological richness of the Brazilian people and in the solutions seen as "poor" in the light of high culture. "It is the *nordestino* leather and empty cans, it is the inhabitant of the 'Villas', it is the black and the Indian, it is a mass that invents, that brings an indigestible contribution, dry, hard to digest."[53]

Beyond factual architecture, the intellectual building developed by Lina Bo Bardi became a reference for many architects in Brazil. Her main disciples, the duo of architects Marcelo Ferraz (1955) and Francisco Fannuci (1952), from the Brasil Arquitetura studio, have traced their path and are clearly linked to the ethical and aesthetic principles formulated by the Italian-Brazilian architect.

The experience of Lina Bo Bardi seems to anticipate, to some extent, the ways of thinking and acting of the current generations of young people, organized in the so-called "architecture collectives". Not only because of her approach to the popular universe but because in many of her works "the hand of the Brazilian people" was directly incorporated with mutual work between architect and labor – as in the *Espírito Santo do Cerrado* church, in Uberlândia (1976-1982). The construction of identities exemplifies a move from historical memory to popular memory.

In the current fragmentary context, many young architects are no longer moved by utopias, but by social awareness and the need to act quickly and together with communities. The work of "architecture collectives" at microscales, sometimes deliberately anti-technological and little specialized, seems to oppose the modern ideology *strictu senso*. However, in the work of this generation, the social sense, the principles of economy, simplicity, and technical reproducibility persist.

Conceiving architecture as a service is a valid way, in tune with a time when great narratives have fallen and in which the idea of individual authorship is questioned. However, the current magnitude of urban and social problems seems to demand more than good and transformative localized interventions. In the modern archive of Latin America, there are very good experiences – of national and regional cooperation – that sought to act on the scale of their urban and territorial challenges, with which contemporary social architecture could establish good and renewing dialogues.

In this attempt to put works and authors in different parts of Latin America into dialogue, many important absences can be found. Truly notable architects and production have been omitted, both because of the intrinsic limitations of a book chapter and the possible ignorance of the author. However, the hope remains that the few and limited examples included have been sufficient to represent the different relationships that the architectures of the last three decades established with the design and intellectual heritage of Latin American modernity – or at least how the author relates them, from a point of view contaminated by the Brazilian experience.

This aimed to investigate questions concerning a historical period that overcame different times, characters, formations, and ideals. On the one hand, this is a chapter definitively closed with the physical disappearance of modern training teachers; on the other, it shows a moment of formulation and consolidation of slightly convergent – and equally divergent – characteristics.

The historical conditions of the 1980s were starkly different from those of today. The favorable economic moment during the "pink wave", which raised the left to power in many countries in the first fifteen years of the twenty-first century, has been buried by the effects of the crisis in the North-Atlantic axis in 2008, a scenario later aggravated by the health, economic and environmental crisis brought by the SARS-CoV-2 virus. At the same time, the shift of the global geopolitical axis towards China seems irreversible, announcing a new multipolar power structure, and calling into question Francis Fukuyama's announcement of the end of history in 1989. Although globalization is not liable to be canceled, the assumption of authoritarian governments, led by far-right leaders in different parts of the globe, try to revive old nationalist illusions – where the aesthetic and architectural debate rarely pass unscathed.

Among so many uncertainties on the horizon, it is highly irresponsible to risk any forecast about the main paths that Latin American architects will follow from now on. But the possible developments would soon resize the meaning of the last three or four decades, even for architecture.

Was the 1990s the beginning of the twenty-first century or will the current decade be the return of the 1920s, considered by many as the starting point of the last century?

Will the succession of *shocks* that plague the world have the power to uncover disruptive vanguards, or will we continue the path of gradual and incremental changes?

These are questions that possibly not even time will answer. At most, they will be the object of new historiographical delimitations, which in vain will try to trap time in systematizations *a posteriori*, as useful as they are fictitious. Modern, postmodern, and contemporary, as questioned, have never been successive times.

It will be better to close with a lesson by the master Lina Bo Bardi: "But linear time is an invention of the West, time is not linear, it is a wonderful entanglement where, at any moment, points can be chosen and solutions invented, without beginning or end."[54]

Notes

1. Caetano Veloso and Gilberto Gil, "Cinema Novo", *Tropicalia* Album, 1993.
2. Verde Zein, Ruth. *Leituras críticas*. São Paulo/Austin: Romano Guerra-Nhamerica, 2018, 217. Translation by the editors.
3. Fernández Galiano, Luís. "Split-Screen." *Projeto Design*, no. 251 (2001): 16-17.
4. Arango Cardinal, Silvia. *Ciudad y arquitectura: seis generaciones que construyeron la América Latina moderna*. Mexico City: Fondo de Cultura Económica, 2012, 449-451.
5. Since 1985, one of the most important instances of debate for architecture has been the Seminars on Latin American Architecture – SAL. For more information, see "Divergent Postmodernism: Waisman and Rossi's Thoughts in the Latin American Architectural Discourse", by Ingrid Quintana (chapter included in the page 18 of this book).
6. Eric Hobsbawm and Terence Ranger, *La invención de la tradición*.
7. Waisman, Marina. "Cuestión de 'divergencia': sobre el regionalismo crítico." *Arquitectura Viva*, no. 12 (1990): 43.
8. Waisman, Marina. O interior da história: historiografia arquitetônica para uso de latino-americanos. São Paulo: *Perspectiva*, 2013, 62.
9. Segawa, Hugo. Arquitectura latinoamericana contemporánea. Barcelona: Gustavo Gili, 2005, 19.
10. Arango Cardinal, *Ciudad y arquitectura*.
11. De Anda Alanís, Enrique. *Historia de la arquitectura mexicana*, 4th edition. Mexico City: Gustavo Gili, 2019, 265.
12. Generally, the works mentioned in this text were designed in collaboration with other professionals. However, only the name of the main architect is cited.
13. Adrià, Miquel. "Teodoro." *Arquine*, 16 September 2016 <https://arquine.com/teodoro/>.
14. López Padilla, Gustavo. *Arquitectura mexicana contemporánea. Crítica y reflexiones*. Mexico City: Editorial Designio, 2009, 180.
15. As an octogenarian, Niemeyer was awarded the 1988 Pritzker Prize. Mendes da Rocha was awarded the same prize in 2006, after which he accumulated all the other main awards in the architectural sphere.
16. According to data from the Oscar Niemeyer Foundation, in the first decade of the twenty-first century Niemeyer developed 41 architectural projects, 22 of which were cultural facilities.
17. Pound, Ezra. *ABC da literatura*, 12th edition. São Paulo: Editora Cultrix, 2013, 39.
18. Díez, Fernando. "Oscar Niemeyer: além da arquitetura." In Tributo a Niemeyer, edited by Roberto Segre, 32-36. Petropolis: Viana & Mosley, 2009, 34.
19. De Anda Alanís, *Historia de la arquitectura mexicana*, 284.
20. López Padilla, *Arquitectura mexicana contemporánea*, 219.
21. Segawa, *Arquitectura latinoamericana contemporánea*.

22. Frampton, Kenneth (1983). "Perspectivas para um regionalismo crítico." In *Uma nova agenda para a arquitetura: antologia teórica (1965-1995)*, edited by Kate Nesbitt, 504-520. São Paulo: CosacNaify, 2006 and Lefaivre, Liane, and Alexander Tzonis (1990). "Por que regionalismo crítico hoje." In *Uma nova agenda para a arquitetura: antologia teórica (1965-1995)*, edited by Kate Nesbitt, 521-531. São Paulo: Cosac Naify, 2006.
23. Waisman, *O interior da história*.
24. Fernández Cox, Cristián. "Modernidad apropiada, modernidad revisada, modernidad reencantada." In *Modernidad y posmodernidad en América Latina: estado del debate*, edited by Cristián Fernández Cox and Enrique Browne, 99-109. Bogotá: Escala, 1991.
25. Browne, Enrique. *Otra arquitectura en América Latina*. Mexico City: Gustavo Gili, 1988.
26. Cavalcanti, Lauro, and André Corrêa do Lago. *Ainda moderno? Arquitetura brasileira contemporânea*. Rio de Janeiro: Nova Fronteira, 2005, 395.
27. Wisnik, Guilherme. "Disposições espaciais." In *Coletivo: arquitetura paulista contemporânea*, edited by Ana Vaz Milheiro, Ana Luiza Nobre and Guilherme Wisnik, 170-181. São Paulo: Cosac Naify, 2006, 174.
28. Milheiro, Ana Vaz. "Coletivo: a invenção do clássico." In *Coletivo: arquitetura paulista contemporânea*, edited by Ana Vaz Milheiro, Ana Luiza Nobre and Guilherme Wisnik, 86-97. São Paulo: Cosac Naify, 2006, 93.
29. Torrent, Horacio. "Los noventa: articulaciones de la cultura arquitectónica chilena." In *Blanca montaña: arquitectura reciente en Chile*, edited by Miquel Adrià, 26-49. Santiago: Ediciones Puro Chile, 2011, 38-39.
30. Mondragón, Hugo. "Manifiestos: argumentos que tensaron el discurso de la arquitectura en Chile. 1990-2015." In *El discurso de la arquitectura chilena contemporánea. Cuatro debates fundamentales*, edited by Hugo Mondragón and Francisco Díaz, 16-24. Santiago: Ediciones ARQ, 2017, 16-17.
31. Alonso, Pedro Ignacio. "Monomaterial: abstracción y técnica en el discurso de la arquitectura chilena contemporánea." In *El discurso de la arquitectura chilena contemporánea: Cuatro debates fundamentales*, edited by Hugo Mondragón, 28-41. Santiago: Ediciones ARQ, 2017, 31-32.
32. Which explains, in part, its international success, crowned with the Pritzker given to Aravena in 2016.
33. Torrent, "Los noventa," 29.
34. Nobre, Ana Luiza. "Prática em comum." In *Coletivo: Arquitetura paulista contemporânea*, edited by Ana Vaz Milheiro, Ana Luiza Nobre and Guilherme Wisnik, 18-25. São Paulo: Cosac Naify, 2006, 20.
35. Iglesia, Rafael. "No sé si lo que hago es arquitectura." *Río Negro* (December, 2006) <http://www1.rionegro.com.ar/diario/tools/imprimir.php?id=4591>.
36. Initial information from the research project Arquitectura del Estado en Argentina – Siglo XXI, by Arroyo at the group of the Observatory of Contemporary Latin American Architecture, Nov. 08, 2021.

37. "Cajas modernas." *Arquine*, no. 33 (2005), 3.
38. Canales, Fernanda. "La modernidad arquitectónica en México: una mirada a través de los medios impresos." PhD diss., Universidad Politécnica de Madrid, 2013, 305.
39. De Anda Alanís, *Historia de la arquitectura mexicana*, 241.
40. Ibid., 266.
41. Adrià, Miquel, and Andrea Griborio. *Radical. 50 arquitecturas latinoamericanas*. Mexico City: Arquine, 2016, 13.
42. Carranza, Luis Eduardo, and Fernando Luiz Lara. *Modern Architecture in Latin America: Art, Technology, and Utopia*. Austin: University of Texas Press, 2015, 333.
43. Alonso, "Monomaterial," 31-33.
44. "Arquitetura como uma forma peculiar de mobilizar o conhecimento", interview with Marta Bogéa, apud Wisnik, Guilherme, ed. *Paulo Mendes da Rocha: encontros*. Rio de Janeiro, Beco do Azougue, 2012, 102.
45. Bucci, Angelo, Ivo Giroto, and Ingrid Quintana-Guerrero. "De abajo hacia arriba: diálogos entre la cultura global, la tradición y la arquitectura contemporánea." *A&P Continuidad* 5, no. 9 (2018): 22-31 <https://doi.org/10.35305/23626097v5i9.181>, 29.
46. Le Corbusier, intellectual father of the first Latin American modernist generation, proposed a careful look at the lessons of the classical past. However, he never explicitly formulated modernity as the result of a synthesis with the historical past, or based on the idea of national identity.
47. Olivares, Rosa. *El ritual del caos*. Madrid: Exit Publicaciones, 2005, 9.
48. Mijares Bracho, Carlos. *Tránsitos y demoras: esbozos sobre el quehacer arquitectónico*. Mexico City: Mehnir Libros, 2002.
49. Canales, "La modernidad arquitectónica en México," 315.
50. Fernando Luiz Lara and Luis Eduardo Carranza consider that the strong regionalist tendencies of the 1980s have been converted into a growing integration between Latin American architects and architectures. An example of the friendly relationship between Bucci, Iglesia and Benítez. Cf. Carranza and Lara, *Modern architecture in Latin America*, 325.
51. Rodríguez Alcalá, Javier. "Notas sobre territorio, ciudad y arquitectura (1870-2019)." In *Arquitecturas contemporáneas en Paraguay*, edited by Goma Oficina, 26-51. São Paulo: Romano Guerra Editora / Editora Escola da Cidade, 2019, 48..
52. Beresin, Pedro, Vitor Pena and Eduardo Verri. "Investigaciones polifónicas." In *Arquitecturas contemporáneas en Paraguay*, edited by Goma Oficina, 52-79. São Paulo: Romano Guerra Editora / Editora Escola da Cidade, 2019, 60.
53. Bo Bardi, Lina. "Tempos de grossura." In *Lina Bo Bardi*, 4th edition, edited by Marcelo Carvalho Ferraz, 210-215. São Paulo: Instituto Bardi / Casa de Vidro, Romano Guerra Editora, 2018, 210.
54. Ibid, 210.

Pacific: Local Materialities and Transatlantic Perspectives
Ingrid Quintana-Guerrero

No country can claim to itself the possibility of America's globality. The only chance of understanding the Pacific is with America as a whole.
Godofredo Iommi, *Dos conversaciones de Godofredo Iommi*.[1]

Introduction

It is paradoxical to designate the Pacific – that erotic sea, in the view of the Argentine poet Godofredo Iommi – as the object of transatlantic intellectual exchanges. It is even more paradoxical to do so regarding the architecture of the South American continent, whose Pacific coast, mostly occupied by Chile, is as diverse as it is fragmented, underused, and even disdained. The latter is the case of the Pacific region of Colombia, a country embraced by two oceans that has turned its back, when it comes to public administration, one of them precisely the Pacific, in contrast to the opening up of the Caribbean Sea. Latin America has not only been interpreted (by others and by itself) from canonical history as the scene of lush Caribbean landscapes but also primarily from its relationship with the West – Europe and North America – through the Atlantic Ocean that connects them physically. Perhaps this is why the cross-sectional views of South American architecture focused on a relationship with the Pacific coast are practically non-existent – even more so if one exclusively investigates its production in the late twentieth century.[2]

Maybe America looks at its extensive Pacific coast as a "gigantic whale" (quoting Iommi again), as a "sign of adventure, death and poetry."[3] In one of his improvised speeches during the construction of Amereida – a city with beaches on Ritoque (Valparaíso region), which is simultaneously a plastic manifesto, poetic expression, and school of architecture – Iommi expressed his disagreement regarding the understanding of Chile as the only door of the Pacific to the world.[4] The Chilean strip is just one of the multiple territories that make up an "inland sea" called America, which depends on the surrounding waters, both to the east and to the west, to exist and globalize. This statement makes sense if one considers that this "inland sea" corresponds to an ancient fragment of Pangaea, confined by a single gigantic ocean (the Panthalassa), which millions of years later was recognized as seven seas.

Amereida was a paradigmatic experience and a creative and pedagogical adventure undertaken by a group of artists, builders, and poets led by Iommi and the Chilean architect Alberto Cruz. Enrique Browne evokes this group's journey from Punta Arenas to Santa Cruz de la Sierra, in Bolivia – center of the Southern Cross constellation – as an act that recognizes a Pacific that is deeper than the continental edges touched by the ocean.[5]

Thus, the term *Pacific* would not refer to a specific geographical location, but to a condition enhanced by the spoken word – in this case, the speeches given by the poet and other journey participants – as the founder of the built object and founder again of the architectural discipline. Besides setting a precedent in the history of contemporary Chilean architecture, Amereida issues a response to the attitude recognized by critics and historians in local architecture. For them, the group of professionals and academics associated with the Seminars of Latin American Architecture – SAL proposed a theory a *posteriori*; a discourse generated from the review of the styles developed in the work of its main participants.

Emancipated Pacific: an Anti-Regionalist Region

The Latin American architectural "emancipation" of identity discourses linked to a regionalist side of postmodernity[6] had its origin, on the one hand, in an international reaction animated by speakers of the Second International Congress on Critical Regionalism (held at the Delft University of Technology in the Netherlands, in 1990).[7] Their declarations

El Errante inn, Ritoque Open City.   Source: Ingrid Quintana-Guerrero, 2019.

were at the antipodes of the aesthetic and metaphysical criteria used by the architects linked to this movement.[8] On the other hand, there was local resistance, in the Chilean case, pivoting around professors such as Teodoro Fernández and Monserrat Palmer,[9] who had a great commitment to heritage intervention and the study of construction technologies, respectively. This defiance was linked to the economic upswing of that country before the resurgence of democracy, at the beginning of the 1990s.[10] Thus, in Chile, the path was opened to project discourses based on material exploration and linked to the technological developments of its growing industry and new understandings of its raw materials.

The intellectual substratum of the projects erected in the southern country dispensed with the academic validation that accompanied the debates in the SAL and established the architectural work itself as a means of "theoretical" dissemination. Thus, young architects launched not only the technical and heritage agenda but also the poetic potential announced by the *phalènes* – as Cruz and Iommi called their *performances* on the territory. Materializing the inns built in Ritoque over the next five years, the leisurely appearance of these austere constructions which blend in with the hardness of the coast, was constituted as a manifesto for new interpretations of human habitation and the relationship between the builder and the matter. For example, in El Errante Inn built in 1994, Manuel Casanuevas used a flexible membrane as formwork, which attributed an unusual plasticity to materials such as concrete. However, according to Roces, this work proposes a more decisive relationship with the environment than its matter, defined as the very essence of the building through the correspondence between its internal unevenness and that of the land, the morphological relationship of the envelope / specific solar orientation and the prevailing winds.[11]

These conditions allude to another characteristic widely exalted by historiography and international criticism regarding Chilean architecture of the 1990s: its close dialogue with the arid landscape of the Pacific coast – a vulgarized debate at the local level, according to Horacio Torrent.[12] For Enrique Browne, it is a reissue of strategies used in the planned site of several state commissions in Chile during the previous decade, which were erected as isolated pieces in the city, under a modern vision of urbanism. In the words of Browne, regarding Amereida, "each building proposes something new and its construction is artisanal,"[13] which announced the main ideas that underpin Chilean architecture at the end of the twentieth century: material exploration and unique location – the latter generally outside the consolidated urban fabric.

However, the silence and irreverence of the Open City, although exceptional, are features of still isolated episodes in recent Chilean architecture, in contrast to the vast set of projects published in the local journal *ARQ*, directed by Palmer from 1980. The house that Mathías Klotz, a young architect from Viñamarino, had built for his mother in the fishing village of Tongoy, in 1991, was the first of the works published in this journal.[14] It endorsed a language closer to the vernacular mountain construction than to the silent eccentricity of the inns. The Klotz house marked a new turning point both in *ARQ* (a sign of its new director's interests) and in Chilean architecture because it opened the way to small-scale works – mostly architects' houses built for themselves[15] with low-cost materials – based on material exploration and extreme formal synthesis. The programmatic flexibility must be added to these arguments, which was already anticipated during the 1980s by the work of emblematic Chilean architects such as Cristián Valdés.[16] The journal *ARQ* ended up becoming the main medium to collect the fundamental ideas of experimental Chilean architecture during the 1990s.

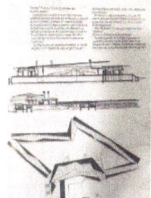

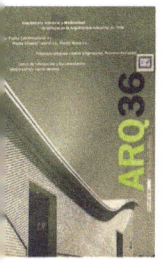

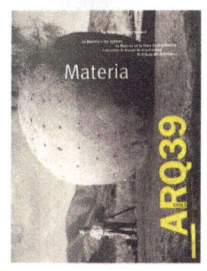

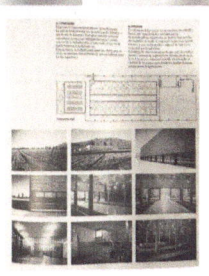

Collage of ARQ publications with works by Klotz, Radic, and other young Chilean architects.

Source: Ingrid Quintana-Guerrero, based on material from the Sergio Larraín García Moreno Documentation Centre, 2022

From Coast to Coast: International Exchange Without Rhetoric

Some authors, such as Fernando Pérez Oyarzún,[17] recognize *ARQ*'s relevance in the emergence of an international exchange of Chilean works, as a non-verbal[18] manifesto of architecture from the south, by promoting their publication in foreign and widely distributed journals. The most notorious example was *The Architectural* Review's publication of the Klotz house in 1999. However, in the competition for the Chilean pavilion at the Universal Exhibition of Seville in 1992, other scholars[19] identified the trigger for an unusual interest in southern architecture from the other side of the Atlantic. The winning architects, José Cruz Ovalle and Germán del Sol anchored their work in the Chilean tradition of timber construction[20] while making a nod to the future by appealing to new and sophisticated industrialized construction techniques. This last element aligns with the architecture teaching at the Catholic University of Santiago, using exuberant forms reminiscent of the Amereida pavilions and contrasting with the "boxes" published in *ARQ*, to the extent that they seek to shape the space, not its container. In short, the uniqueness of the pavilion lies in its double condition of continuity and rupture, besides being a commercial showcase in favor of its nationals, adapted to the laws of the global market, since recent local policies promoted hiring their services abroad.[21] Although Cruz Ovalle voluntarily departed from the precepts taught at the school of Valparaíso by his uncle Alberto Cruz, he materializes in this and other works a discourse articulated by terms such as corporeality and subjective experience.[22] Where appropriate, the written word does not precede the constructed object; in fact, it is avoided as a strategy to strip architecture of any will to represent or figurate. We will come back to this.

It is striking that despite the distance of Cruz Ovalle and other architects with constant representation in *ARQ* – such as Mathías Klotz, Smiljan Radic, or Teodoro Fernández

The Boy Hidden in a Fish. Installation by Smijlan Radic and Marcela Correa at the Architecture Biennale di Venezia, 2010. Source: Dalbera, Wikimedia Commons.

– from the academic discourse, the visibility of Chilean work and ideas in the Anglo-Saxon and contemporary European architectural scene was consolidated in part through educational institutions. Rodrigo Pérez de Arce, trained at the Architectural Association of London by the Krier brothers, then returned to Chile with a deep interest in enhancing the experimental character of the Valparaíso school through workshops between both institutions.[23] His interest was replicated with the new millennium arrival and the search for young talents by institutions such as Harvard's Graduate School of Design – GSD (led by its chairman, Chilean Jorge Silvetti), with a discourse based on phenomenological aspects, among others. Sebastián Irarrázabal and Alejandro

Aravena stand out among these young people. From a very early stage of his professional practice, Aravena developed a consistent discursive practice – inaugurated with the writing of *Los Hechos de la Architectura* (The Facts of Architecture).[24] This was endorsed years later worldwide when he was awarded the Pritzker Prize and the Silver Lion, at the Biennale di Venezia of 2008 – Smijlan Radic also exhibited his work at this event in 2010. Both his work and ideas and those of his colleagues have also been disseminated locally, although already with international projection through the cultural platform *Constructo*, founded in 2008 by Jeanette Plaut and Mauricio Sanovic.[25]

The main discursive lines, commonly used by these and other renowned Chilean architects during the transition between the twentieth and twenty-first centuries, dialogue with art and the autobiographical. The same happens with the form/technique relationship – condensed into mono-material architecture according to Alonso[26] – and the landscape, referring not only to desolate landscapes[27] dramatically exalted by tourist infrastructures but also to the re-foundations or new readings and responsibilities of the urban public space.[28] These are findings of a research team from the Catholic University of Chile, led by Hugo Mondragón, for whom the constructed manifestos of the last 25 years in Chile "seem dominated by a wide universe of figures; namely, the primitive cabin, Malevich's supremacist desert, ships and planes, furniture and costumes, vernacular, weaving, povera art, and Land Art."[29] This statement holds the keys to differentiate the recent Chilean architectural thought from that which characterized the 1980s scene. The works from these figures are abstracted from their political context,[30] which goes beyond the debates opposing the dictatorship.

Continuous Surface and Ancestral Footprints: Peruvian Networks

Chile and Peru briefly experienced similar historical circumstances that led to similar project concerns in their mountains and on their coasts. A military dictatorship[31] arose in the Inca country during the 1990s, which caused a time lag regarding the socioeconomic phenomena impacted by the complex political climate in its southern neighbor. Therefore, the absence of a state interest in financing public works limited the architectural reflection of the private sphere. The Lima disciplinary circle had benefited from Juvenal Baracco's legacy – one of the few Peruvian participants in the SAL and responsible for the postmodernist indoctrination of several generations of architects in his country. His beach houses had an undeniable vernacular vocation.[32] They were a tool to establish the language derived from the traditional tectonics assimilated by Baracco and to contrast with the volumetric forcefulness and structural boldness of the works of his Chilean contemporaries. Their implementation would have put in crisis the solid North American postmodern apparatus (in Peru the crusade for a critical regionalism made little impact[33]), which sustained the most relevant architectural production of the Peruvian scene during the turn of the century by the hand of professionals such as Emilio Soyer.

According to Wiley Ludeña Urquizo, in the mid-1980s *Sendero Luminoso*'s period of violence caused structural changes in Peruvian urban society, reinforced by the subsequent insertion of the neoliberal model.[34] Here, a generational change began with the help of Arquidea, a group of young graduates from the Ricardo Palma University of Lima, which ventured into the design of public space through significant local competitions. They made an unprecedented effort to consolidate an architectural intellectual culture in the Peruvian capital – "lethargic by isolation and crisis"[35] at that time – through conferences, exhibitions, and publications. Its founders, Juan Carlos Doblado, Javier Artadi, and

José Ortego (later joined by Jean Pierre Crousse) openly reacted to the prevailing postmodernism in their country and called themselves *modernists in a rational sense*.[36] The formal influence of the New York Five in their production is evident, a product of Baracco's academic teaching.[37] They also absorbed certain dissemination tools from the New York context, such as an exhibition of beach houses, which consolidated these commissions as the main architecture laboratory on the Lima coast during the end of the previous century. This was a similar program to the experimental houses in Chilean architecture,[38] although faced with different climatic conditions since the Peruvian coast is a desert without wind, rain, or drastic thermal oscillations.

Although Arquidea dissolved in the early 1990s, its legacy was the call to ideas as the foundation of practice. For example, Juan Carlos Doblado ventured into journalism through chronicle and architecture criticism with a column in the newspaper *El Comercio*, in 1986. Javier Artadi[39] fed his project repertoire by observing the pre-Columbian traces in Chan Chan or Puruchuco – already studied and highlighted by Emilio Soyer[40] who was attracted by the "minimalist" aesthetics of these ruins. Contemporaries outside this group, such as Elio Martuccelli, contributed with global concerns characteristic of the cosmopolitan view of his generation's graduates.[41] Martuccelli,[42] who has a Ph.D. from the Polytechnic University of Madrid, points to the individuality of the architectural object as a cultural event representative of society and proposes the notion of *fragment* as a natural condition of the specific reality in Lima,[43] capable of articulating a modern architectural discourse adjusted to the local scenario. This connects material operations such as tarrajeo – consistent with the scarcity of resources and technical skills in certain Peruvian regions – with design strategies derived from a high architectural culture. According to Doblado, the *tarrajeo* – a stereotomic technique found in the pre-Hispanic ruins – gives rise to the continuous surface,[44] frequently used

Place of Memory, Lima. Barclay and Crousse.

Source: Ingrid Quintana-Guerrero, 2019.

in beach houses that, in contrast, are based on basic tectonic principles.

The beach houses, identified by international professionals as the genuine expression of Lima architecture,[45] have been criticized by Ludeña for whom these constructions are mostly anchored: "a kind of annoying minimalism as contradictory as the unimaginable coexistence between the architecture of transparencies, voids, and economy of defects with the twisted and baroque culture that radiates from power, this new emerging middle class. [...] the Creole acquires the true meaning of urban expansion: a minimalism of lies."[48]

Besides this disapproval, Cynthia Watmough,[47] Guillermo Málaga,[48] and Miguel Rodrigo[49] contribute to a culture of

House in Playa Bonita, Alexia León.   Source: Hugo Segawa, 1998.

criticism and self-criticism that may be the main differentiating factor of Peruvian architectural thought during the 1990s, compared to the Chilean. But let's concentrate on the main integrating element of both approaches: geography, although not mentioned by poetry but by history. In reference to Jean Pierre Crousse's beach houses in La Escondida (in partnership with Sandra Barclay), he describes his actions after his return from France, resulting from the confrontation with the territory and the millenary indigenous presence. "The foremost theme in everything we have done is the interpretation of the place in its territory. We make an architecture of the place, of our time, sometimes, hopefully, of all times."[50] This supposes a departure from the architecture of the purely formal exploration, by the composition based on a solid visual culture, consistent with the work of Radic or Alberto Cruz.

Interestingly, with Barclay and Crousse's French career, contemporary Peruvian architecture acquired notoriety on the other side of the Atlantic, by winning the Europan Ideas competition[51] – the first of a series of awards granted to the Peruvian couple in the old continent, including the Mies Crown Hall Americas Award. Alexia León also had a successful international career, being nominated frequently for international architectural distinctions. León worked as a professor in the architecture workshop led by Juvenal Baracco at Ricardo Palma University until 1996. In her professional practice, she has supported her research on housing design in the Peruvian coastal desert, where part of her projects are based. Her house on Playa Bonita (1998, published in *ARQ*, Chile, and finalist in the second edition of the Mies van der Rohe prize) displays horizontal architecture with a continuous envelope. Here, the domestic condition is explored with a programmatic specificity greater than that of her Chilean colleagues, conceived from the Peruvian culture of inhabiting (with typologies such as the patio) and the idea of different levels of shelter and indoor/outdoor relationships.[52] The return to democracy[53] and the beginning of the third millennium ignited the transatlantic dissemination of Peruvian architecture, with an emphasis on its coastal production. This has intensified in recent years within the regional context thanks to initiatives such as Tectura, a series of meetings organized by Doblado with a group of South American architects whose works are not necessarily on the Pacific coast but the same "inland sea."[54]

Colophon: Other "Pacifics"

After the previous review and the reminder of the Pacific's transcendental role as an "inland sea", it is worth enquiring what is our final take on the Latin American Pacific condition, transferable to other geographies in the south of the continent. Torrent provides a clue, describing a group of architects of the late twentieth century as representative of a new Latin American stage, "maybe without heroes. [...] there is no coherent generic discourse in [their architectures], [...] they do not demand attention, they become present for daily life."[55] Therefore, the "pacific" attitude of the South American architectural activity (here homologous with the first meaning of the word in the Royal Spanish Academy dictionary,[56] absolutely opposed to the political tension caused by dictatorships) starts from its argumentation away from a doctrinal imposition and with a deep understanding of the shared problems, which are not global but concerning the ordinary citizen in Latin America. This is a discourse constructed from the bottom up, fed by the ways of inhabiting our cities.[57] Torrent's prediction is an alien condition to the work presented in the previous lines: an urban confrontation. The same author identifies spatial examples built by Solano Benítez or Rafael Iglesia, who privilege constructive exploration, in intermediate cities hundreds of kilometers from the Pacific coast (e.g., Chiloé, Piura, Rosario, and Asunción) and far from the great South American metropolises.

Like the research of their Chilean and Peruvian colleagues, this evades rhetoric centered on a language of universal certainties in favor of a corporeal consciousness and constructive tradition, now within consolidated urban fabrics.[58] With this, they partially vindicate the intuition of Kenneth Frampton in defense of critical regionalism, stating that "an architect can achieve a small act of autonomy by adhering to a poetics of structure."[59] We add to this "realistic" position, of greater theoretical ease, that many "pacific" architectures propose a common strategy: an approach to the architectural elements that become more complex to relate to the terrain[60] and the public.

Finally, although the South American inland part of the continent is the one advancing more towards the Atlantic, the authors of architecture emerging in Brazil are tuned with their colleagues' project spirit in the Pacific. The two strengthened relations thanks, among other factors, to the return to democracy for the "colossus of the south" in 1985 and the establishment of the Mercosur treaty in 1991. Carranza and Lara,[61] regarding the Universal Exhibition in Seville in 1992, identified again the competition for the Brazilian pavilion design as the modern hegemony reaffirmation both in its form syntax and use of concrete – the structure of the unexecuted proposal comprised a pre-stressed beam of approximately forty meters, simply supported by two side walls. Beyond its formal economy as a visual identity of Brazilian architecture, the manifest character of the winning project for Seville lies in the openness to regional dialogue. Its authors, Angelo Bucci and Álvaro Puntoni engaged in a dialogue, perhaps unintentionally, that provoked a renewed interest in the modern Brazilian masters on the other side of the Atlantic.[62] To some extent, the Brazilian pavilion in Seville – which exalted the audacity of the masses of concrete supported by scarce and slender *pilotis*, typical of the São Paulo tradition – aspired to become the foundation stone of the interregional and transcontinental exchange established two years later in the formal meeting of Latin American architects, during Lisbon's celebrations as the Ibero-American capital of culture.[63]

Postscript: Back to *(Val) Paraíso*[64]

Enrique Browne concluded his reflection about Ritoque as follows: "Perhaps unintentionally, the architects of the Open City can bring to light values in what today only seem precarious and aggregative works of necessity. If so, these values could be translated into works of architecture. That would be a very American [very Pacific!] and contemporary contribution."[65]

From the experimental rooms of the Amereida to the small-format works conceived by the "golden architecture generation" exponents in Chile, the architectures of the Pacific consolidate research that emphasizes the elementality of its existence. In other words, its physical presence rejects any will to represent and exalts the contemplation of its paradisiacal environment. In his book from 2004, *Hacia una nueva abstracción*,[66] José Cruz Ovalle exposes with few words this search, which apex is the construction of the campus for the Adolfo Ibáñez University in Valparaíso (2010-2011), a few kilometers from Ritoque:

> for the first time the artistic transcendence of a work takes place as the perfection of its immanence; the work sings in the presence of what is there, before our eyes, without referring us to what is outside, beyond, through its representation. With this, abstraction opened a radical change: it freed the eye from that prior representation of what precedes the first look. [...] a new abstraction in the sense that admits degrees, not that universal abstraction proposed by the avant-gardes that were heading towards its consummation in the idea of a single totality like that city that experienced Neoplasticism.[67]

This new confrontation of Cruz Ovalle with the *Porteño* (Valparaíso) landscape means his return to the geographical and conceptual origin of his experimentations, with a relevant intermediate step in Santiago in the construction of the same university's campus in the capital. In both examples, it is possible to identify a succession of pavilions connected and adapted to the hillside, which is not only an adequate response to the discarded topography of the place, but an opportunity to promote fortuitous encounters that enhance daily life on campus: "area of collective development of its environment, away from commercial symbolism or constructive repetitions, which simply weaken daily functionality. [...] In this way, it evokes vernacular situations, with a sense of the activity that provides an adequate shelter, as well as cultural projection."[68]

Thus, the habitual and everyday life becomes the center of a discourse that, appealing to abstraction as its main resource, ignores itself as discursive. This condition is ratified by the campus built by Cruz Ovalle for the same university in the mountains of Santiago.

This last reflection and the illustrated scenario led us to question whether the architecture of the Pacific – regardless of its time and latitude – is generally and deliberately autistic – minimalist, as Ludeña referred to his Peruvian compatriots' works – in contrast to the prolific oratory of its architects – so celebrated in the "Global North" – and the growing exchanges between them. We question whether the architecture is deliberately topographical – even if it is on the beach or in the mountains – and whether it is deliberately domestic (despite its program) due to its physical consciousness and human scale. To verify this, it remains to examine the ideas and works produced along thousands of kilometers on the Pacific coast, between Mexico and Ecuador.

Adolfo Ibáñez University Campus in Santiago, José Cruz Ovalle.

Source: Ingrid Quintana-Guerrero, 2019.

Notes

1. Iommi, Godofredo. *Dos conversaciones de Godofredo Iommi.* Viña del Mar: Taller de Investigaciones Gráficas, Escuela de Arquitectura UCV, 1984.
2. We have reiterated the absence of parallel studies that problematize the lines of argument of the end-of-the-century regional architecture, in contrast to the number of studies about local areas. This gap is more noticeable in the Latin American Pacific. In Chile, there are abundant works that question this relationship nationally from contemporary design discourses (the most outstanding, without a doubt, are the coordinated by Hugo Mondragón in 2017 and the compendium of *ARQ* articles cited below). However, there are few attempts to engage in transnational dialogue from this lens. They do so tangentially (if not coincidentally) in the works of Roces, José Luis. "Elogio de las sospechas." In *Forma y Materia: Un Mapa de la Arquitectura Latinoamericana Contemporánea*, edited by Griselda Bertoni. Santa Fe: Ediciones Universidad Nacional del Litoral, 2012 and Plaut, Jeannette and Marcelo Sarovic. *Pulso 1 / Pulso 2: nueva arquitectura en latinoamérica.* Santiago: Constructo, 2012 / 2014. reviewed for this chapter, as well as the Tectura series of colloquiums, organized in Lima by Juan Carlos Doblado in 2014 and described in this text.
3. Iommi, *Dos conversaciones de Godofredo Iommi*, 2.
4. Ibid.
5. Browne, Enrique. "Amereida: una experiencia arquitectónico-poética chilena." *Summa*, no. 218 (1985): 74-83.
6. The term *critical regionalism* was first coined by Alexander Tzonis and Liane Lefaivre, and rapidly associated with architectural postmodernism. However, for Hugo Segawa it is pleonasm to speak of postmodern architecture in Latin America. Our subcontinent is in essence postmodern, as shown by their more iconic examples of regional architecture (even that called modern), which propose a rupture from the synthetic language of the hegemonic modernity in architecture. Segawa, Hugo. La *Revista Projeto y las conexiones latinoamericanas.* Conference in Universidad Nacional de Colombia, February 1, 2022.
7. "According to literary critic Frederic Jameson, postmodernism, despite its exaltation of variety, remains a homogenizing cultural force capable of absorbing all differences and forms of resistance and transforming all forms of reality into simulacra. In this way, the critical quality of a supposed critical regionalism is questioned from the moment in which the production of architecture cannot avoid its dependence on the system. In other words, critical regionalism can easily be colonized by postmodernism [...]. Another problem presented by the possibility of a regional resistance to the postmodern condition in the less developed parts of the world is that it could exclude these populations

from the promise of market welfare and universal suffrage that has been partially achieved." Ingersoll, Rand. "Un paréntesis para el regionalismo crítico." *Summa*, no. 281 (1991): 10-11.
8. Some texts that advised the need for this distancing from the regionalist discourse at the South American level have already been mentioned in the presentation of this book, including those of Segawa, Hugo. *Arquitectura latinoamericana contemporánea*. Barcelona: Gustavo Gilli, 2005, and Torrent, Horacio. "Cristal opaco: la arquitectura latino-americana como categoría historiográfica." In *Sudamérica moderna*, edited by Hugo Modragón and Catalina Mejía, 276-290. Santiago: Ediciones ARQ, 2015. Of this last author, it is also worth mentioning the article where he stated: "The construction of totalizing discourses resulted in the eclectic works, which populated the panorama during the 80s. Paradoxically, Latin American historiography has for years recycled those great successes, sometimes in a triumphalist tone, sometimes for its criticism and revision in the dialectic of one's own and that of others. These discourses would contribute little to the layout of freer and more fruitful paths and would fall into the invention of 'adjective' formulas about our appropriate modernity, made our own or resented." Torrent, Horacio. "Al Sur de América: antes y ahora." *ARQ*, no. 51 (2002): 10-13 <http://dx.doi.org/10.4067/S0717-69962002005100007>, 12.
9. Mathías Klotz, quoted by Mondragón, Hugo. "Manifiestos: argumentos que tensaron el discurso de la arquitectura en Chile. 1990-2015." In *El discurso de la arquitectura chilena contemporánea. Cuatro debates fundamentales*, edited by Hugo Mondragón and Francisco Díaz, 16-24. Santiago: Ediciones ARQ, 2017.
10. It is well known that this "Chilean economic miracle" took shape long before the fall of the Augusto Pinochet government, with the interference of the Chicago Boys in the inclusion of neoliberal policies and the decentralization of the economy: a model put into practice by United States in the southern country, which meant a break with the regional model and its Andean Pact. This fact influenced the proliferation of public work and positions during the 1980s, both in Santiago and in other Chilean cities. Hugo Mondragón, interview with Ingrid Quintana-Guerrero, Nov. 2019. Unpublished.
11. Roces, "Elogio de las sospechas."
12. In an interview with Ingrid Quintana-Guerrero, Nov. 2019. Unpublished.
13. Browne, "Amereida," 79.
14. *ARQ*, no. 23 (May 1993).
15. During this phase, the absence of the State is notable, both financially and providing guidelines. According to Torrent in "Al Sur de América," this absence could have influenced the fact that the 1990s work lacked the magnificence of those of the modern heroic period.

16. Regarding the Urregola house by Cristián Valdés and José Antonio Prado, it was said in the journal *Summa*: "The volumes with clear features and the open floor plan – which refers to statements of the Modern Movement – offer flexibility to adapt to programs and internal changes; its materiality expresses what Cristian Valdés states about the purpose of a project: to create a shed, a general structure that allows different life systems to be accommodated, whether that of a school, a doctor's office or an office." "Pertenencia y poética latinoamericanas." *Summa*, no. 251 (1988): 72-77, 72.
17. In an interview with Ingrid Quintana-Guerrero, Jul. 2019. Unpublished.
18. Probably the exception to this is the habitation-house of Smiljan Radic: "it is the text that accompanies the publication of the work which, without trying to explain it, ends up completing it and charging it with meaning. This design technique that is nourished by autobiographical events and that operates through the multiplication of project languages (writing, photography, sculpture, drawings) has been taken to its ultimate consequences by Radic, who is the author of a considerable number of works with a desire to manifesto." Mondragón, "Manifiestos," 19.
19. Carranza, Luis Eduardo, and Fernando Luiz Lara. Modern *Architecture in Latin America: Art, Technology, and Utopia.* Austin: University of Texas Press, 2015; Mondragón, "Manifiestos."
20. According to Horacio Torrent in an interview with Ingrid Quintana-Guerrero, Nov. 2019. Unpublished.
21. Humberto Eliash, in an interview with Ingrid Quintana-Guerrero, jul. 2019. Unpublished.
22. José Cruz Ovalle, in an interview with Ingrid Quintana-Guerrero, Jul. 2019. Unpublished.
23. Fernando Perez Oyarzún, in an interview with Ingrid Quintana-Guerrero, Jul. 2019. Unpublished.
24. In reference to the essay included in the book with the same name published in 1999, with Fernando Pérez Oyarzún and José Quintanilla. The latter was Aravena's professor at the Catholic University. In this text, Aravena addresses the phenomena that give architecture a physical body: gravity, the slippery nature of water, the human traces of the landscape, etc. Cf. Aravena Mori, Alejandro, Fernando Pérez Oyarzún, and José Quintanilla Chala. *Los hechos de la arquitectura.* Santiago: Ediciones ARQ, 2007, 13.
27. "Its main areas of development are associated with the management, promotion and dissemination of Latin American architecture, design and art and contemporary points of convergence, a space that includes research, publications, seminars, curatorship and development of national exhibitions and international architecture, design and art." *Constructo.* "Quienes somos" <https://constructo.cl/quienes-somos/>.

28. Alonso, Pedro Ignacio, Umberto Bonomo, Macarena Cortés, and Hugo Mondragón. "El discurso de la arquitectura contemporánea chilena: cuatro debates fundamentales." *Rita: revista indexada de textos académicos*, no. 7 (2017): 54-59 <https://doi.org/10.24192/2386-7027(2017)(v7)(01)>, 20. Among the Chilean works of the 21st century that simplify the mono-material, Ibid., 31, includes those by Pezo von Ellrichshausen (Casa Poli, 2005), Rafael Hevia, Rodrigo Duque and Gabriela Manzi (Faculty of Economics and Business of the Diego Portales University, 2014) and Alejandro Aravena (Anacleto Angelini Innovation Center, 2014), among others.

27. Macarena Cortés evokes a series of works that obey to this nature characterized by providing tourists luxury services in extreme places and by promoting them as a counterpoint to the landscape and a human refuge. Among the works discussed is the Hotel Tierra Patagonia by Cazú Zegers (2011), the Explora Atacama by Germán del Sol (2018) and the Hotel Tierra Atacama, by Matías González and Rodrigo Searle (2007-2008). "In all these cases, the place, the landscape and the location appear inalienable, where the forms extended in the territory use strategies that combine complex geometries and references to local conditions". Alonso et al., "El discurso de la arquitectura contemporánea chilena," 57.

28. This is the contribution by Umberto Bonomo to the theoretical panorama behind public works in Chile after the return to democracy: by introducing the Italian term *consapevolezza* – awareness – the author points out the role of these works in the vindication of architecture as an event with the potential to transform society and culture. This includes both emblematic interventions in public space – for example, the Palacio de la Moneda Cultural Centre, by Christian Undurraga – and public social housing operations such as Quinta Monroy de Elemental. Alonso et al., "El discurso de la arquitectura contemporánea chilena," 45.

29. Ibid., 23.

32. Horacio Torrent, "Los noventa: articulaciones de la cultura arquitectónica chilena."

33. We refer to the prolonged government of Alberto Fujimori, after the self-coup d'état that took place in 1992. This dark period of Peruvian history is remembered for the high levels of corruption and the influence of Vladimiro Montesinos in State decisions. There was also a liberal economic restructuring that took place in Peru based on the Chilean experience. Ludeña Urquizo, Wiley. "República, sociedad y arquitectura en el Perú contemporáneo: entre el compromiso y la evasión social." In *50 años de arquitectura peruana: libro de oro de la arquitectura peruana*, edited by Carlos Cosme Mellarez, 82-98. Lima: Colegio de Arquitectos del Perú, 2013.

34. Among these are the Marrou-Yori houses (1985), the Gezzi house (1985) and the Gasteña Sarmiento houses (1985).
35. The little Peruvian architecture affiliated with the concept of regionalism found radical criticism. "It is an architecture that, in the key to a critical regionalism devoid of critical sense, has had no other destiny than to become a predictable formal cliché. Transformed into replicable fashion, the trivialization of its primary pre-existence, as Gillo Dorfles would say, would finally mean its own 'death.'" Ludeña Urquizo, "República, sociedad y arquitectura en el Perú contemporáneo," 92.
36. "With the *Sendero Luminoso* central command dismantled in September 1992, five months after the self-coup and neutralized in the countryside by the peasant patrols, political stability contributed to the economic stability that consolidated privatization, neoliberalism, and the open insertion into globalization. The unprejudiced opening to the market quickly revealed the enormous gap between our country and not only central countries but even our own neighbors. [...] Undoubtedly, the compulsive, chaotic and uncontrolled process of subdivision (outside of any regulation and comprehensive plan for metropolitan development) and urbanization of the coast is the best expression of the brutal return to that liberal city of savage nineteenth-century capitalism that fostered the Fujimori decade: a city without laws and regulations, without order and consensus, without a sense of citizenship and common good, apart from laws and the order that governs the economy of maximum profitability and disregard for the inclusive city for all." Ibid., 92.
37. Ibid., 92.
36. Doblado, quoted in Bryce, Patricio, Moris Fleischman, Diego Franco, Héctor Loli, and Jorge Sánchez. *ConPosiciones: 20 aproximaciones a la arquitectura peruana*. Lima: Nómena, 2010.
37. Ludeña Urquizo, "República, sociedad y arquitectura en el Perú contemporáneo."
38. "We have to consider that they are very small projects, with reduced programs and land, in some cases spectacular." Watmough, quoted in Bryce et al., *ConPosiciones*, 148.
39. "The city of Chan Chan always caught my attention, that architecture is so continuous, so perfect. Then we have the colonial architecture that is built with plastered *quincha* [...]. I think this is the hallmark of Peruvian coastal architecture." Artadi, quoted in Bryce et al., *ConPosiciones*, 144.
40. Quoted in Bryce et al., *ConPosiciones*, 63.

41. As in the Chilean case, the connections between Peruvian contemporary architecture and the world were made through international educational institutions such as the Architectural Association, where David Mutal completed his undergraduate studies with a research project started at the Ricardo Palma University. Enrique Ciriani worked for Frank Gehry and later had a notable teaching career in France. Cf Bryce et al., *ConPosiciones*. Years later, at the Catholic University of Chile and GSD Harvard Alexia León collaborated with Jorge Silvetti in the course GSD1319: Copán Archaeological Museum and built temporary partnerships with renowned international firms, including Herzog and De Meuron. Cf. Eráusquin, Mariangela. "Alexia León Angell 1970." *Un día / una arquitecta, segunda temporada*, September 20, 2016 <https://undiaunaarquitecta2.wordpress.com/2016/09/20/alexia-leon-angell-1970/>.

42. Martuccelli, Elio. *Arquitectura para una ciudad fragmentada: ideas, proyectos y edificios en la Lima del siglo XX.* Lima: Universidad Ricardo Palma, 2000.

43. René Poggione expresses the impossibility of referring to a proper Peruvian architecture because of the diversity of this country and the absence of great schools. "In Chile and Argentina, there is also more competition and therefore the standard is better, and we are interested in the standard, because it makes cities." Poggione, quoted in Bryce et al., *ConPosiciones*, 150.

44. "It can be a slab or a wall using plastering. It is certainly different from using an exposed brick wall with a wooden ceiling: therefore, using different pieces and materials. There is an aesthetic relationship with the pre-Hispanic structures that are still standing, which were made of adobe." Doblado, quoted in Bryce et al., *ConPosiciones*, 149.

45. "Some foreign architects have told me that when they look at these little beach houses — white, pure, and geometric — they see something that I had never thought about: they are tremendously from Lima. What do they mean? Suddenly, a certain way of living in summer in a certain socioeconomic sector makes them from Lima." Martucelli, quoted in Bryce et al., *ConPosiciones*, 147.

46. Ludeña Urquizo, "República, sociedad y arquitectura en el Perú contemporáneo," 92.

47. "There is a lot of talk about beach houses because they are on display, but there are also houses in the city that are very interesting only hidden by walls." Watmough, quoted in Bryce et al., *ConPosiciones*, 148.

48. "Beach houses seem interesting to me and there are great examples. Now, there are 100 houses, of which five are good and 95 copies of others or have no greater value. The density in which they are implanted in the ground takes away many possibilities. When you see other houses facing the sea, isolated, it is about the house and its surroundings. Here the beach houses are attached to 50 others, in that sense, it loses a lot of quality." Málaga, quoted in Bryce et al., *ConPosiciones*, 148.

49. "Deep down we don't have Peruvian architecture because we don't have our own ideas and that is precisely where we have to go. [...] creating your own architecture today in a highly technological global world demands being involved in multiple investigations with the presence of international patents of a highly cultural level in all fields of knowledge. We settle for choosing solutions in a catalogue." Rodrigo, quoted in Bryce et al., *ConPosiciones*, 150.

50. Crousse, quoted in Bryce et al., *ConPosiciones*, 144.

51. "Our proposal was that architecture could reveal the urban fact, put it in evidence. We call this concept "urban revealer" because we were interested in showing the specific qualities of the site, which are often hidden or not visible at first sight. And we won." Ibid., 85.

52. Ludeña Urquizo, Wiley. "Vivienda, hogar y ciudad: autonomía y límites en la arquitectura de Alexia León." A: Revista de la Facultad de Arquitectura y Urbanismo 2, no. 3 (December, 2008): 94-124.

53. "Supported by an international economic scenario, a period of stability began, with greater growth dynamics, starting in the new century, with the expulsion of the corrupt dictatorship, after a determined collective action to recover democracy." Beingolea del Carpio, José. "Medio siglo de sinuosas intermitencias arquitectónicas: 1962-2012." In *50 años de arquitectura peruana: libro de oro de la arquitectura peruana*, edited by Carlos Cosme Mellarez, 25-80. Lima: Colegio de Arquitectos del Perú, 2013, 56.

54. The participants of the different versions of Tectura include Giancarlo Mazzanti, Mauricio Rojas and Felipe Mesa, from Colombia; Mauricio Rocha, Michel Rojkind, Javier Sánchez, Alberto Kalach from Mexico; Solano Benítez and Javier Corvalán, from Paraguay; Felipe Assadi, Sebastián Irarrázaval and Ricardo Abuauad, from Chile; Angelo Bucci and Marcelo Ferraz, from Brazil; Jaime Ruillon, from Costa Rica; Marcelo Gualano, from Uruguay; Javier Artadi, Juan Carlos Doblado, Luis Longhi, David Mutal and the Barclay and Crousse Studios, 51-1, Llosa-Cortegana Arquitectos y Nómena, from Peru. Cf. "Congreso TECTURA 2014, Lima / ¡Sorteamos un cupo!" *ArchDaily Colombia*, September 18, 2014 <https://www.archdaily.co/co/627385/congreso-tectura-2014-lima-sorteamos-un-cupo>.

55. Torrent "Al Sur de América," 12.
56. Calm, peaceful, that does not cause fights or discord.
57. Bucci, Angelo, Ivo Giroto, and Ingrid Quintana-Guerrero. "De abajo hacia arriba: diálogos entre la cultura global, la tradición y la arquitectura contemporánea." *A&P Continuidad* 5, no. 9 (2018): 22-31 <https://doi.org/10.35305/23626097v5i9.181>
58. "Today when the discourse unity has been broken, how can we achieve an architecture that is susceptible to as many interpretations and meanings as history itself, that denies the narrative discourse as a closed whole, that can be told in a thousand ways, where narrative loses meaning [or] interpretation. That does not establish any truth or falsity [...] an architecture that is willing to shed its certainties, that measures itself with what it does not know, that ventures to follow more diffuse clues, even false clues, that takes risks, that is encouraged to walk outside its conceptual network." Rafael Iglesia, quoted in Torrent, "Al Sur de América," 13.
59. Quoted in Ingersoll, "Un paréntesis para el regionalismo crítico," 11.
60. Plaut and Sarovic, *Pulso 2*. Alluding to a much more recent context, Plaut and Sarovic highlight this strategy in the Pachamanca house (51-1 Arquitectos, 2008-2009). This is "a private house in the arid and fragile landscape of Lima, a city in which each new construction generates more stress in an overpopulated metropolis that witnesses a dramatic competition for basic resources such as drinking water."
61. Carranza and Lara, *Modern Architecture in Latin America*.
62. Paulo Mendes da Rocha is the most notable case. His first publication outside Brazil was in: Adrià, Miquel. "Arquitectura latinoamericana." *2G: revista internacional de arquitectura*, no. 8 (1998): 4-13 <https://dialnet.unirioja.es/ejemplar/189909>.
63. Solano Benitez, in an interview with Ingrid Quintana-Guerrero, Nov. 2019.
64. Paraíso in Spanish means Paradise.
65. Browne, "Amereida," 41.
66. The text was later published in Cruz Ovalle, José. "Para una nueva abstracción." *ARQ*, no. 70 (2008): 19-21. The quote is taken from that edition.
67. Ibid., 20.
68. García Alvarado, Rodrigo. "El nuevo campus de la Universidad Adolfo Ibáñez: equipamientos para una vivencia significativa." *Dearq*, no. 11 (2012): 82-93 <https://doi.org/10.18389/dearq11.2012.09>, 89.

Materializing Imaginaries: Local Knowledge and Idiosyncrasies
Ingrid Quintana-Guerrero

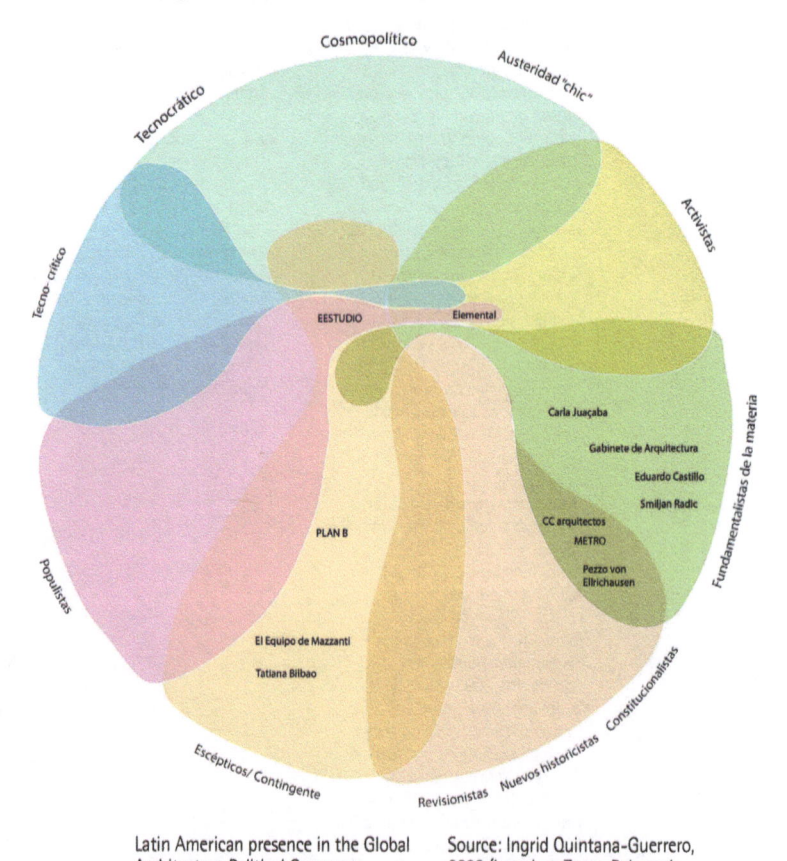

Cosmopolítico
Austeridad "chic"
Tecnocrático
Activistas
Tecno-crítico
EESTUDIO
Elemental
Carla Juaçaba
Gabinete de Arquitectura
Eduardo Castillo
Smiljan Radic
Fundamentalistas de la materia
PLAN B
CC arquitectos
METRO
Pezzo von Ellrichausen
Populistas
El Equipo de Mazzanti
Tatiana Bilbao
Constitucionalistas
Escépticos/ Contingente
Revisionistas Nuevos historicistas

Latin American presence in the Global Architecture Political Compass.

Source: Ingrid Quintana-Guerrero, 2022 (based on Zaera-Polo and Fernández-Abascal, 2016).

Introduction

The Spanish critic Alejandro Zaera-Polo identified a series of contemporary architecture discursive universes, which are illustrated with the Global Architecture Political Compass. This diagram included a few Latin American actors, who were placed in the interstices of these universes, in categories such as "Material Fundamentalists",[1] "Populists" and "Skeptics/Contingents." In the words of Zaera-Polo, these last two categories are similar in their conceptual simplification – away from functionalist positivism –, discourse and image mediatization via the Internet, newspapers, and other alternative media.[2] This criticism is shared by Alfredo Brillembourg and others, who denounce the current proliferation of architects who act more as producers of media content than buildings.[3]

These trajectories are not that interested in the specific problems of the discipline – resulting in less consistent architectures constructively, such as those by the Mazzanti or Frida Escobedo teams, among others –, but rather in the exploration of new formats to disseminate ideas, which include games, cartoons, etc. In contrast, Zaera-Polo describes an "Activists" category.[4] This seeks alternative modes of management and research that focus more on the real social transformation possibilities offered by architecture than on the application of new technologies and the creation of compositional strategies. This category highlights positions predominantly recognized on the subcontinent, such as a dialogue between recent architecture and the knowledge and values of people who have inhabited the Latin American territory for centuries and whose idiosyncrasy was severely altered by the European physical and intellectual colonization.

On the threshold of the twenty-first century, mestizo imaginaries – including controversial features within their contemporary socio-economic systems – acquired relevance in different Latin American cultural products. In the case of architecture, disciplinary research oriented by mutual learning incorporates architectural discourse and plural conversation with the project's users[5] and other professionals. Besides, it integrates ancestral knowledge into constructive processes and the efficient use of available physical and human resources,[6] in tune with a holistic (and imperative!) idea of sustainability. To a greater or lesser extent, these attitudes redefine the objectives and essence of the architectural craft. They are not completely new as participatory construction experiences and research on local techniques had already been promoted since the 1960s and 1970s, respectively, with the training programs of the Inter-American Centre for Housing and Urban Planning – CINVA[7] and with the work of Álvaro Ortega[8] as a consultant to the UN. However, at the dawn of the third millennium, this redefinition has become the conceptual basis for most of the production of a subsequent generation of architects in less visible countries in Latin American disciplinary historiography. On a continental scale, it established itself not just from the formal theoretical production but from the development of international academic meetings[9] and the special emphasis given to this phenomenon in prestigious architecture biennials.[10]

In the following lines, we will discuss some recent practices that seek to vindicate Latin American architecture, in particular the Andean, produced on the margins of the formal, in the *inmundo*.[11] This architecture uses two broad categories that are transversal to the work and the ways of thinking about architecture for many architects and contemporary collectives in Latin America. These are the translations of habits and meanings typical of the idiosyncrasy where these practices take place – facilitated by dialogue with the communities that receive the architecture –, which is unusual in regional studies and the adaptation of ancestral knowledge to available construction techniques and current needs.

Collective Thinking and Community Architecture

The Argentine researcher Alejandro Crispiani[12] identifies a series of common attitudes in young architects of the early twenty-first century, who define themselves as facilitators, managers, and apprentices in the building cycle, whose actions are part of a process of defense and construction of the territory. Among these attitudes, and within the full exploration of architectural construction possibilities, has developed what the Paraguayan architect Solano Benítez describes as *cum-versar*.[13] This entails meeting on-site with all the stakeholders around a specific and real problem and solving it by "spinning it around" collectively, discussing materializing alternatives.

That is precisely the type of conversation – a discourse that is not recorded in major treatises but in the memory of its interlocutors – that guides the action of architecture offices serving lacking communities in countries such as Paraguay, which recently had visibility in international architectural criticism. The voice of these communities is fundamental in the processes of architectural conception and execution, through professional training in construction processes and the transmission of traditional knowledge in tune with current sustainability criteria. This exchange – massively extended to other countries in the region – requires adapting the disciplinary representation codes to be understood by the public and incorporating typical factors of the inhabitants' daily lives within the narratives defining the project, regardless of its scale. Therefore, the architect's discourse takes a back seat, becoming an echo of its recipient's voice.

An example of this point of view, with urban effect, is the *Pescaíto* operation, in a popular neighborhood in Santa Marta – capital of the Magdalena department, on the Colombian Caribbean Coast. This city is known for being the place where the legendary local footballer Carlos "El Pibe" Valderrama grew up and emerged as a professional player.

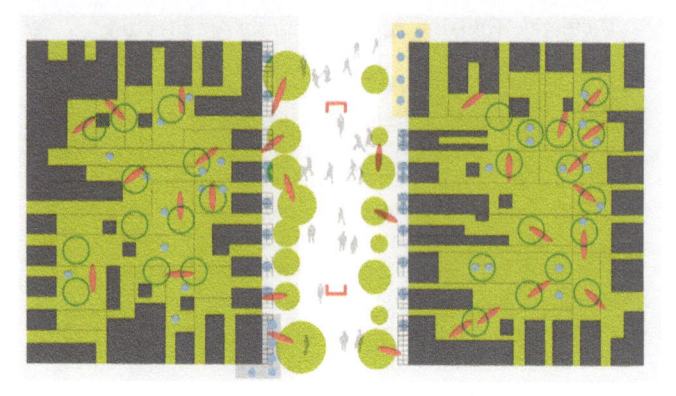

Live plans of Pescaíto.   Source: Simón Hosie, 2017.

This neighborhood intervention, developed in 2017, was financed by the Colombian State, managed by singer Carlos Vives from Santa Marta, and coordinated by architect Simón Hosie from Bogotá. In 2009, for the Casa del Pueblo (People's House) project in El Salado (regions in the Carmen de Bolívar municipality, in the north of Colombia), Hosie had already developed a methodology close to ethnographically named *planos vivos* (living plans). It refers to the construction of cartographies that illustrate the spatial and experiential community relations within the physical and geographical space, which were the basic input for the intervention.[14] The history and physical structure of El Salado were marked by a massacre carried out by paramilitary groups in 2000. The objective of that intervention was re-signification for the few inhabitants who returned years after fleeing the homicidal violence at the center of the municipality. Hosie and the survivors drew living plans of El Salado, in which they recorded the routines and rituals of the community and then self-built the Casa del Pueblo project.

In the *Pescaíto* operation, the living plans promoted "a dialogue – full of contradictions and conflicts – between different approaches to urban problems; it is supported by

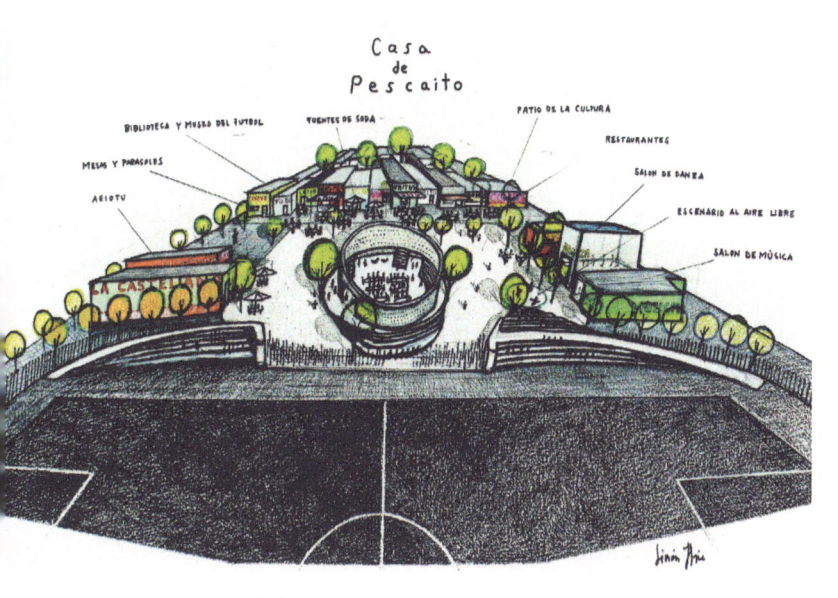

Pescaíto House.
Source: Simón Hosie, 2017.

knowledge from scientific and academic disciplines, but, at the same time, it rescues the value of local experience formed over generations."[15] The team led by Hosie identified an architectural acupuncture strategy as appropriate for the transformation of the surrounding environment, with small-scale operations that re-established the connection between the seaport and the neighborhood. This allowed the community to re-appropriate its public space – streets and football fields – for sports and festive purposes left behind after internal social conflicts. Even with the design of urban furniture, Hosie enhances these practices, baptizing objects with colloquial names that refer to banal day-to-day activities, which subverts the meaning of the words. For example, "hamadora" proposes a play on words between *hamaca* (hammock) and *mecedora* (rocking chair) but also alludes to *amar* (to love). Another word was "callejera" (from the street), whose pejorative connotation is associated with prostitution, but in *Pescaíto* it also means a *microfútbol* soccer goal. Microfútbol (street football) is a game that has been elevated to the condition of ritual by the neighborhood's youth – and a *banca* (bench) in public space.

Concurrently but differently to the Colombian state-supported commissions (which tend to repair a vulnerable fraction of the population), the creation and representation of projects with deprived communities in Ecuador have been supported by independent collectives. These are occasionally in partnership with educational centers, challenging the nature of their study programs, which are often disconnected from contingencies in the most sensitive sectors of the population. Enrique Villacís, partner of the Ecuadorian Architecture Office *Ensusitio* and co-coordinator of the project course *Con lo que Hay* (with what is available) from Faculty of Architecture, Design and Art of the Pontifical Catholic University of Ecuador – PUCE FADA, highlights the need to turn the project into a real and more present university experience. Latin American architects are traditionally trained to act in formal contexts, which cover just 30% of the possible field of action.[16]

Therefore, seventh and eighth-grade undergraduate architecture students in PUCE FADA (with some support from schools in Germany, Costa Rica, the United States, and other countries) are advised by *Ensusitio*'s professionals. This happens in an itinerant workshop focusing on a series of needs and communities, which so far has developed throughout seventeen versions in Ecuador and abroad. The students oversee all the necessary processes to materialize the proposal, from the financial management, the organization of community participatory workshops, and the work on site. These are small-scale interventions feasible to implement in one or a few school periods. Finally, the projects are disseminated through simple manuals, with brief texts and didactic illustrations that transform the architectural

Cocoa Interpretation Center in Santa Rita (Ecuador).
Source: PUCE-FADA, Ensusitio, 2015.

discourse into simple instructions for the execution of the work by the community, without the help of third parties.

One of the most famous interventions of *Con lo que Hay* is the Cocoa Interpretation Centre in Santa Rita (Ecuador), sponsored by the chocolate industry Paccari.[17] Besides working with Quichwa Indigenous, there was a recognition of the technical potential of local materials in Santa Rita, including the stones that served as foundations. The experience of *Con lo que Hay* inevitably feeds *Ensusitio* practice in projects such as *Casa de Meche* (2016-2017). Again, with the support of Paccari, this project comprised low-cost productive housing for Meche, a cocoa worker who (like many others) lost her humble home during the 2016 earthquake in Ecuador. The objective of *Ensusitio*'s intervention was not to conceive the project but to train Meche and her neighbors (all dependent on cocoa cultivation) to adopt good

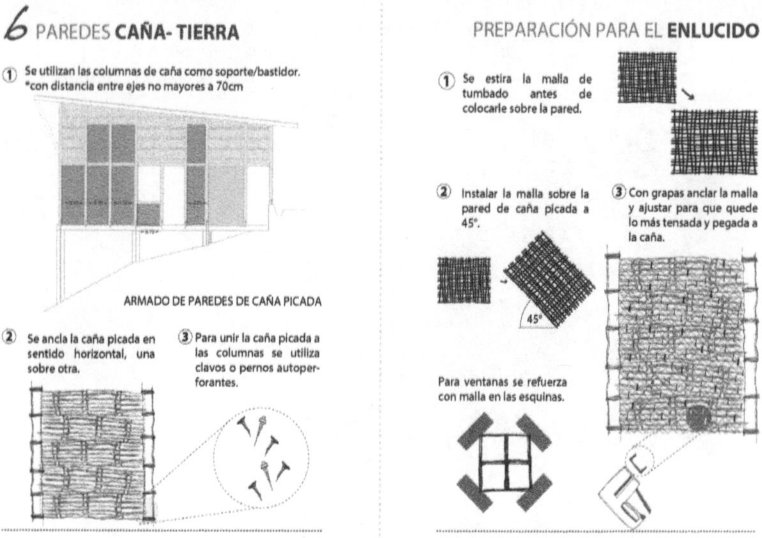

Image of the publication Casa de Meche, taller de buenas prácticas (Meche's house, workshop of good practices).

Source: PUCE-FADA, Ensusitio, 2016-2017.

construction practices and actively participate in the reconstruction of their homes (*Ensusitio*, 2016-2017). Through workshops given by the architects and endorsed by the PUCE FADA, the community was trained in construction techniques with bamboo and rammed earth.

The combination of practice and academia also characterizes the work of *Palomino: sociedad en construcción* (Palomino: Society Under Construction) in Colombia and *Entre Nos Atelier* in Costa Rica. Their organizers take advantage of the university courses that they teach to refine their discourse regarding the true mission of the contemporary architect. As part of their teaching activities at the Pontifical Javeriana University, a group of architects formed by Santiago Pradilla, Antonio Yemail, Daniel Feldman, and the Spanish collective Zuloark has worked at La Guajira, a region

Bathroom Calixto 2. Palomino: sociedad en construcción (2010-2013). Carlos Hernández Correa + PEI Professors: Antonio Yemail Cortés, Christiaan Job Neiman, Santiago Pradilla Hossie, Daniel Feldman Mowerman. + Guest Professors: Colectivo Zuloark – Manuel Pascual, Juan Chacón.
Source: Juan Chacón.

in the Caribbean coast devastated by corruption and drug trafficking. In Palomino, a population with extreme levels of poverty and vulnerability, teams of students learn from the inhabitant's local construction techniques and other knowledge known as "collective intelligence" and carry out mappings to trigger a larger-scale urban and social analysis. Subsequent research focuses on the representation of these inputs.[18]

Thanks to these activities, small infrastructure prototypes – such as dry toilets – were built to encourage environmental awareness and compensate for the absence of basic sanitation networks, as well as the effects of global warming in the region – La Guajira is, paradoxically, a deserted region next to the sea.

The *Entre Nos Atelier* has received commissions such as the design of an infrastructure network for children called CECUDI. In these structures, the assembly of wooden pieces prevails over metallic elements – only used for the roof structure –, as well as overlays made with alternative recycled materials, such as cardboard rolls. The optimization of physical resources follows with the replicability of the constructive elements and the simplicity of their assembly since the process is recorded in a manual of future builders.

Recycling, still timid in *Entre Nos Atelier*'s work, becomes the center of the discussion in several constructive experiences led by the *Futura Natura* collective in Babahoyo, Ecuador, a city near a river with the same name close to Guayaquil. Here, the community joined forces to turn a house into a center of worship (2020), which also functions as an enclosure to host other community integration activities. The architects developed an extremely simple project, recycling as much material as possible from the demolished house on the site for the center of worship.

The new building can accommodate activities such as games and workshops, bringing street life into the building. The narrow budget for the project did not limit its ritual dimension, fundamental in the Latin American idiosyncrasy where Christianity operates as a means for cultural syncretism. In this prayer house, a zenithal light was created to provide the space with a reminiscent atmosphere.

Recycling awareness, very strong in the work of *Futura Natura*, is also explored as a philosophy of life by the Ecuadorian collective *Al Borde*. In their *Casa en Construcción* (House under Construction, 2014), architects and students – as the project was part of an academic workshop – rehabilitated empty spaces and reused existing materials on an old site, giving them a new life cycle. For example, old tires were used for the new roof, and stones from the old construction to reinforce the foundations. They also left room for spontaneous vegetation growth.

Al Borde's projects generally center their debate on the real impact of architecture on the daily lives of the neediest communities. With this work, they criticize the use of money as the only viable resource for the materialization of architecture, appealing instead to the economy of exchange. Thanks to this, their achievements acquire a particular appearance, often an unfinished look – an allegory to the *Povera* aesthetic, according to some critics. Therefore, the house is also an architectural manifesto, later revisited in the installation *Dark Resources* presented by *Al Borde* at the 2016 Architecture Biennale di Venezia, curated by Alejandro Aravena, demonstrating that it is possible to solve urgent needs only with the available means.

Collectives and other organizations led by learning and construction with and for communities with scarce resources have also emerged in countries such as Mexico[19] and Venezuela, formulating actions where the building is not the center of the thinking process. In Caracas, there are several groups such as the international collective Urban Think Tank and *AGA Estudio*, whose recognition and dissemination of legal and illegal occupations in abandoned buildings constitutes a declaration of other possible fields of action in the contemporary architecture world.

In the first case, the Torre David – internationally renowned due to the exhibition "Torre David / Gran Horizonte" at the 2012 Architecture Biennale di Venezia – describes a process of self-management, derived from the occupation of the unfinished tower and its consolidation as a vertical *favela*. Urban Think Tank was not a direct actor in the occupation but a witness, using it as a scenographic instrument to incite a discussion about design authorship and the seductive ability of the architect to offer a dazzling vision of a possible future, in contrast to the built space reality. This is a more vibrant "anti-project" than fictitious projects by professional teams. [20]

In the second case, Casino by *AGA Estudio* proposes the appropriation of an abandoned building in the center of Caracas. It was originally intended for leisure and illicit activities (pimping) and was later expropriated by the Venezuelan government because of the gambling prohibition. The building functions today as a "self-managed and cooperative social equipment between organizations of emerging creators."[21] It is an ecosystem in which different manifestations of cultural economies and practices develop daily and spontaneously in the public space, such as "skating", on the cover of the *Casino* aided by pop-up devices. This obeys a popular logic of "open source" self-determined urbanism, in which the occupation precedes the intervention, ratifying *AGA Estudio*'s argument about the right to the city as an infrastructure for life.[22]

In the context of informality, *AGA Estudio* has also developed hybrid projects – self-management and processes accompanied by professionals – with a systemic vision to generate impact throughout parts of the city. This is based on three basic rights.[23] the right to know, the right to decide, and the right to do. These are the three pillars of intervention, such as Catia 1100 in 2015, projected on the eastern border of the Venezuelan capital and adjacent to a national nature reserve. According to local current urban regulations, the height limit for a building is 1100 meters above sea level.

Catia 1100, construction process of Plaza Estacional Square.

Source: José Bastidas, 2015.

AGA Estudio and their associated collective, Pico, joined the community's efforts to collect material and recruit labor to improve collective housing – considered as such because they are closely attached and share foundations. Additionally, it created intermediate resting spaces for pedestrians whose houses are inaccessible by vehicles. These pedestrian areas acquired a particular character as spaces to contemplate the Caracas urban landscape.[24]

In the previous lines, the role of Paraguayan architects was tangentially mentioned in the positioning of a much more horizontal and, perhaps, anonymous way of thinking about architecture. Although this matter is addressed in greater depth in another section, it is emphasized here that such alternative architectural manifestations have been brewing in that country since the early twenty-first century, led by architects such as Javier Corvalán. The Aqua Alta collective, a group of outstanding young architects and national and foreign students (mainly Italians, and involving Corvalán),[25] was created with the initial purpose of building the Paraguayan pavilion for the 2014 Architecture Biennale di Venezia. It currently promotes sustainable development through public, social, and cultural projects focusing on the environment – which is its primary emphasis –, the public, and the communities invested in resolving problems affecting their territory.

Aqua Alta acts within rural and urban interstices through research on training, design, and construction processes, in constant dialogue with peer regional organizations. Among its interventions was the development of a system of emergency bridges to deal with a series of severe floods in Asunción in 2016.[26] These were easily replicable structures thanks to construction manuals disseminated through social networks. Despite its vocation to attend to the urgent needs of the population, the collective's philosophy is nourished by the relevance of water in the city's physical infrastructure – this is deduced from the collective's name and the intervention mentioned – and by its symbolic value within the local culture. This culture transcends the young Paraguayan democratic history supported by its indigenous roots, which are more alive than in neighboring countries, thanks to the strength of their native language within contemporary idiosyncrasy.

Between the Ancestral and the Everyday

Countries with ethnic diversity such as Colombia or Brazil, derived from a greater plurality of indigenous people who occupied these extensive territories long before the first European colonization, contrast with the Guarani context. Here, the *inmundo* is not reduced to a mestizo imaginary – understood as the white and indigenous mix – but to a dialogue between other ethnicities, frequently in a context of segregation, due to a greater slave trade migration from Africa. In Paraguay, Solano Benítez labels several architectural practices working at the limit of the discipline's legal margins within the current country's condition as "pirate"[27] – in reference to the prominent role of smuggling in its economy.[28] In Colombia, this association encompasses the scars from the previous century left in its territory by violence and drug trafficking.

The *Saberes Ancestrales* educational park emerged in Vigía del Fuerte (Colombia) as a response to this. Awarded at the Quito Pan-American Architecture Biennial (BAQ 2014), this work deals with a double condition of cultural and geographical isolation and social marginalization. Vigía del Fuerte sits on the border between two contrasting regions, Antioquia and Chocó. Antioquia is one of the richest Colombian departments with significant industrial development; its capital (Medellín) is recognized for its recent social urbanism improvements. Chocó is a department in the Pacific region abandoned by the Colombian State and with the highest rate of Afro-descendant population in the country. The lack of institutional presence in this area, its impenetrable geographical condition – this humid jungle known as the Darien Gap and bordered by the Atrato River is only accessible by helicopter – and its location near the Atlantic and Pacific Oceans made this territory a strategic place within the drug trafficking routes.

The *Saberes Ancestrales* project team was coordinated by architects from Medellín working with the Antioquia government and led by Diana Herrera Duque. It also had the participation of the community that, in addition to the social stigmatization caused by drug trafficking, remains anchored in time due to the condition of the Palenque and *Embera* indigenous reservations. The new infrastructure comprises a simple structure of two open pavilions, responding not only to a school program but also to the customs and collective activities of the Zamba community (a mixture of indigenous and black populations). They live in stilt houses on the water, permanently seeking protection from the sun and wind; hence the use of woven screens as main facade elements.[29]

This search for shading is also found in recent works by young Paraguayan architects, emulating a condition of traditional Guarani architecture known as *ma'era*. In private and domestic scale buildings projected in that country, by *Elgue Estudio* (e.g., a health center in Villa Olivia in 2006 and medical clinic and housing in 2016) or by Sonia Caríssimo and Francisco Tomboly (Dúplex in 2010 and Vivienda Pajarera in 2015, both in Luque), shading is achieved with alternative devices to the typical eaves that predominate in indigenous architectures. For example, ceramic lattices and large overhangs over habitable areas on the ground floors, among other resources that allude to the narrative established by their precursors Benítez and Corvalán regarding the recycling of the available main building material – brick – extracted from demolitions.

Back in Colombia, Antioquia has undoubtedly been one of the most internationally known regions in the last thirty years due to the actions of the extinct Medellín Cartel, but also because of its status as an architectural laboratory. Many of the city's innovative facilities, such as the Parque de los Pies Descalzos and the Unidades de Vida, were developed by the architecture department at Empresas Públicas de Medellín – EPM, the largest provider of public services in Colombia owned by the Mayor's Office. Among its social responsibility programs is Aldeas EPM – selected for the 2020 Colombian Biennial of Architecture and Urbanism – created to build rural schools; some benefitting the Embera community in the Puerto Rico region. Through a series of participatory workshops, the indigenous community representatives opted for a typology of two pavilions with a centralized layout, typical of indigenous constructions known as "tambos," and for materiality that alternates textile elements with a wooden structure using resources from the forests managed by EPM around its dams.

The Embera Chamí is one of the surviving indigenous languages, spread along the Pacific coast in Colombia. Other millenary cultures, such as the Zenú – also known as Sinú – are present in the regions near the Antioquia and Chocó departments, as well as in the Córdoba department in the Atlantic region. The Sinú share with the Embera the knowledge of a manual craft: weaving. Their famous arrow cane woven fabric, used for the "vueltiao" hat, is considered part of the national heritage. This knowledge spread to the interior of Colombia, where there was greater extermination of the indigenous population. There, other communities inherited the craft of weaving, also promoting the use of wicker, a fiber of Spanish origin.

Artisans from Nocaima, a town in the Cundinamarca department, worked on the construction of the Casa Tejida, designed again by Santiago Pradilla in collaboration with the Spanish collective Zuloark. The proposal challenged the conventional housing program – comprising a holiday home for wealthy clients – by configuring continuous spaces like those in rural housing. Besides, Pradilla went beyond traditional production by appealing to wicker artisans such as Doña María, whose fabrics are normally used for smaller objects. She and other artisans received training to expand their know-how for the benefit of the construction. The added value in the Casa Tejida was the creators' sustainable awareness because the carbon footprint of the materials and transport was minimal. This attitude shows the understanding of individuals committed to the idea of austerity typical of the *inmundo*.[30]

In the Colombian projects presented so far, the action within the margins mentioned by Corvalán for the Paraguayan context also alludes to the suburban and rural environments in which the projects are built.[31] This is the case in the Colombian coffee region, which extends throughout the western cordillera (a branch of the Andes Mountain range that penetrates the south of the country) and was colonized by Antioquia's white communities. There subsists a culture and aesthetic typical of coffee farmers, characterized by the construction in *guadua* (bamboo) and adobe.

Indigenous people from the Paez community, in the archaeological region of Tierradentro (Cauca department) in the south of Colombia, used to work in coffee plantations before being forced out by drug cartels who replaced their traditional crops with coca crops. Simón Hosie, a recent graduate at that time, was interested in anthropology and lived with the Paez community for several months. They asked him to help construct a community center in the town of Guanacas (known as Casa del Pueblo since 2004) to restore the social fabric, broken because of the gradual urbanization and the incidence of drug trafficking in their territory. Hosie and the community worked on the conception and construction of the center – which was later transformed into a library –, appealing to traditional techniques from the coffee region, although without the romanticized language that characterizes Antioquia's colonization architecture. Its centralized typology directly alludes to Paez's worldview and the observation of nature, which explains the numerous activities held in the building, in parallel to its library program, such as training and recreational activities.[32] The functional versatility of architecture in this and other projects shows the use of ideas emerging from the collective, from the bottom up.

Final Considerations

The work of the architects presented above accounts for a generalized material consciousness; although it uses the same digital and audio-visual media of architects identified as "Material Fundamentalists" and "Populists" – appealing to Zaera-Polo's categories – to disseminate their achievements and procedures and to summon individual action. Through the transgenerational meanings of the constructed-from, and the processes of physical resources transformation based on popular knowledge, community dialogue is created by professionals who see themselves as a piece in the engine materializing architectural space. In this order of ideas, the discourse of the architect – who never operates alone – is stripped of sophisticated concepts and words and concentrates its ideas on the constructed object, its execution process, and the social dynamics it generates.

It is worth noting that many of the examples mentioned here were collected thanks to the concept of *minga*, a Quechua word that expresses collaborative social work. This would explain why some interventions cling to their indigenous past, in the form of "countervalues" of global culture, where ostentation, easy money, and the desire for spontaneous fame govern the functioning of many contemporary professionals. The architecture designed by and for the collective contributes to the materialization of imaginaries as diverse as geographies in our subcontinent: a territory occupied by a multiplicity of people, mostly of aboriginal roots, who not only share problems detonated by segregation and poverty but also the deep sense of solidarity that drives them to work as a community.

Notes

1. In this category, the ideas of Chileans such as Smijlan Radijc stand out, whose synthetic approach to form is explained by the exploration of local construction techniques, as we described in another chapter in this book.
2. Zaera-Polo, Alejandro. "Ya bien entrado el siglo XXI ¿las arquitecturas del post capitalismo?" *El Croquis*, no. 187 (2016): 253-287, , 252; 270.
3. Brillembourg, Alfredo, Hubert Klumpler, Alexis Kalagas, and Michael Waldrep. "Architecture in the Age of Digital Reproduction." *Journal of Visual Culture* 15, no. 3 (2016): 349-356 <https://journals.sagepub.com/doi/10.1177/1470412916665145>," 349.
4. Zaera-Polo, "Ya bien entrado el siglo XXI ¿las arquitecturas del post-capitalismo?", 257.
5. Benítez, Solano. "Universos en tensión." *Summa+*, no. 173 (2019): 10-12, 10.
6. Corvalán, Javier. "Un fin del mundo: fragmento de el libro negro." *Rita: revista indexada de textos académicos*, no. 1 (2014): 40-43 <http://ojs.redfundamentos.com/index.php/rita/article/view/39/30>, 43
7. Peña Rodriguez, Martha Liliana. "El programa CINVA y la acción comunal." *Bitácora Urbano Territorial* 12, no. 1 (2008): 185-192 <https://revistas.unal.edu.co/index.php/bitacora/article/view/18621>, 185-192.
8. See Ortega, Álvaro. *Álvaro Ortega: prearquitectura del bienestar*. Bogotá: Escala, Universidad de Los Andes, McGill University, 1989.
9. Regarding these meetings, it is worth noting that although many have taken place within undergraduate courses in different faculties throughout Latin America, most of them have been managed by architecture groups or by temporary societies. In the case of the reviews prepared by the academy, "Informal Means: Alternative Design Practices in Latin(x) America," organized by the Harvard Graduate School of Design, stands out. See: <https://www.jchs.harvard.edu/calendar/informal-means-alternative-design-practices-latinx-america>. It brought together significant experiences from the first two decades of the twenty-first century. When reviewing the conversations of this meeting, "the term participatory architecture is on the rise within the practices and theory of recent architecture." Díaz-Osorio, Myriam Stella. "Arquitecturas colectivas y participación como estrategias para la construcción de ciudad latinoamericana." *Revista de Arquitectura* 21, no. 2 (2019): 3-11 <https://revistadearquitectura.ucatolica.edu.co/article/view/2670>,

6. Thus, the architect goes from being an individual creator to an interpreter. However, the same author acknowledges that "little has been theorised about the ways in which these exercises are carried out, a situation that contrasts with the increase in recognition, events and the strengthening of practices in the real scenario." Ibid., 11.
10. The most notorious (and perhaps controversial) case has undoubtedly been that of the Quito Biennial, which central theme was "The useful classroom", focused on the approach of practices with a tangible impact on the immediate context. Cf. Dueñas, Natalia; Teresa Pascual, eds. *Catálogo académico de la XX Bienal Panamericana de Quito.* Exhibition Catalogue. Quito: Colegio de Arquitectos del Ecuador Provincial Pichincha, 2016, 6.
11. This aphorism by the Paraguayan architect Javier Corvalán refers to the cultural universe outside the Western *mundus* (world), on the margins of the mainstream. It is based on architectural thought and experimental practice connected with the cultural and geographical roots of the project. Corvalán, "Un fin del mundo," 40.
12. Quoted in María Victoria Silvestre and Claudio Solari, Silvestre, María Victoria, and Claudio Solari. "Exploraciones en el campo de la constructividad: arquitecturas de Rafael Iglesia y Solano Benítez." *Dearq,* no. 25 (July, 2019): 74-85, 75.
13. Benítez, "Universos en tensión," 12.
14. Hosie, Simón. "Casa del Pueblo: nuevo centro de El Salado." *Dearq,* 19 (2016): 104-111.
15. Simón Hosie, *Planos vivos Pescaíto. investigación participativa y diseño sostenible,* 16.
16. Villacís, Enrique. "En el marco del curso 'From The South: pensar arquitectura hoy'." Bogotá: Universidad los Andes, May, 2021 [Talk with students].
17. Quintana-Guerrero, Ingrid, and Rafael Ernesto Méndez Cárdenas, eds. Ethos de la arquitectura latinoamericana: identidad, solidaridad, austeridad. Memorias de una exposición. Quito: Centro de Publicaciones de la Pontificia Universidad Católica del Ecuador, 2018.
18. Yemail, Antonio, and Carlos Hernández Correa. *Palomino: sociedad en construcción.* Bogotá: Pontificia Universidad Javeriana, 2013, 10.
19. See "Third-Nature Architecture for the Solidarity Landscape of the Interior in México. An Approach from its Contemporaneity," by Fabricio Lázaro Villaverde and Edith Cota Castillejos (chapter included in the page 146 of this book).

20. "What is then the role of the architect in this situation? The answer to this question is not simple and thus there was a huge debate in our team as to what would be exhibited. In the end, the conventional architectural drawings ended up on displays on several old televisions dumped on trolleys at the back corridor of the installation, a dry conscious decision. For us, it was time to display another type of architect, one who puts forth a discourse on one billion slums in the world" Brillembourg quoted in Kallipoliti, Lydia. "Torre David / Gran Horizonte." *Journal of Architectural Education* 67, no. 1 (2013): 159-161 <https://www.tandfonline.com/doi/full/10.1080/10464883.2013.767137>, 159.
21. Visconti, Gabriel. "En el marco del curso 'From The South: pensar arquitectura hoy." Bogotá: Universidad los Andes, November 10, 2021 [Talk with students].
22. Ibid.
23. Besides the right to the city, pointed out by Henri Lefebvre (1975) and embraced by the Venezuelan.
24. Aga Estudio Creativo, *Plaza Estacional*.
25. *Aqua Alta* has more than thirty active members, including Lukas Fúster, Andrea Castellani, Carlos Irigoitia, Fernando Szmuc, Marco Ballarin, Laura Ferres, Joaquín Corvalán, Katja Kostrencic, Paula Stella, Francisco Tomboly, Sebastián Blanco, Simone Cadamuro, Sonia Carísimo, Oliviero Comincini, María Bertha Peroni, Jesús Pereira, Jessica Goldenberg. Cf. Verri Lopes, Eduardo. "Aproximações sobre arquitetura paraguaia contemporânea." Master Thesis, Universidade Estadual de Maringá, Paraná, 2016 <http://repositorio.uem.br:8080/jspui/handle/1/3375>, 9.
26. Santos, Natalia. "Acqua Alta: proyectos paraguayos que flotan en el agua." *La Nación*, January 5, 2016 <https://www.lanacion.com.py/2016/01/05/aqua-alta-proyectos-paraguayos-que-flotan-en-el-agua/>.
27. Ibid.
28. Benítez, "Universos en tensión." Cf. Quintana-Guerrero, Ingrid. "Inmundo: Architectural Metaphors from the Edge of the World." In *Metaphorical Practices in Architecture. The Making of Architecture, Identities and Methodologies*, edited by Sarah Borree, Stephanie Knuth, and Moritz Röger. Londres: Routledge, 2023.

29. Herrera Duque, Diana. "Territorios de la colectividad." Ciclo de diálogos *habitar América Latina*, diálogo 05, ciclo 02. Rio de Janeiro: Red BAAL/UIA, 2021 <https://redbaal.org/territorios-de-la-colectividad/>.
30. Quintana-Guerrero, Ingrid. "Austeridad: austeridad en la arquitectura latinoamericana: un camino por el siglo XX y una perspectiva finisecular." In *Arquitectura latinoamericana contemporánea*, edited by Inés del Pino and Fernando Carrión Mena, 72-83. Quito: Flacso, 2021.
31. Corvalán, "Un fin del mundo," 42.
32. Hosie, Simón. *Planos vivos: arquitectura y comunidad*. Ciclo de conferencias de las artes. Bogotá: Universidad Nacional de Colombia, 2019.

Third-Nature Architecture for the Solidarity Landscape of the Interior in Mexico: an Approach from its Contemporaneity

Fabricio Lázaro Villaverde
Edith Cota Castillejos

Introduction

From the beginning of the twenty-first century, the academic and professional practice of architecture in Mexico has been reunited with a social vocation generated by the crisis of the Mexican Revolution (1910-1917). In the following decades, this allowed the emergence of professionals determined to observe and interact with the social peripheries. This active participation approach was the product of the architects' insertion in the impoverished, urban, and rural realities of Mexico and Latin America, where another architecture was emerging in opposition to the academia and elite institutions.

It is right in the interstices of that field of action, expanded by the frenzy of capital and its urban impact, the *terrain vague* – metropolitan, urban, and rural –, where practices of austerity, and collective and horizontal architecture generate academic *performance*. In Mexico, this scenario builds collective frameworks of the third nature, which, according to Hannah Arendt,[1] is responsible for moving towards adaptive action within the stressed crisis. In this sense, Rory Hyde from Australia mentioned the emergence of new roles in the social practice of architecture.[2] Despite this guideline, the potential of habitat management and social practice has also resulted in the *pro-bono* work of consolidated workshops that seek balance in their media portfolios. However, within this "glocal" inertia, there are notable social actions that come from a full recognition of the contribution that architecture has to social evolution. Therefore, it is essential to analyze and configure individual and collective practices, beacons of a variety of opportunities, as the context for the possible and fair practice of emancipatory architecture in México.

The context of the observation of the community practice of contemporary architecture in Mexico comes from an interest in solving the pressing housing needs of the population since the first decades of the twentieth century. Therefore, nowadays works are re-valued, such as the *Manual del Campesino* (1936) by Víctor José Moya and Ramón Galaviz, published by the Secretary of Public Education – SEP, which emphasizes rural constructions. Moreover, the 1958 *Cartilla de Vivienda*, an initiative by the Mexican architect Félix Sánchez Baylón (1915-1969), was published by the Mexican Institute of Social Security – IMSS with the support of the Pan American Union. This is a popular and free tool aiming to guide people without technical knowledge in the execution of popular housing through basic knowledge of construction, building orientation, alternative construction systems, calculation, and topography.

However, its influence was greater than initially expected since it became reference material for architecture students and especially for their first construction practices in peripheral urban or rural areas. These published works preceded the *Instructivo Sanitario de la Comisión Constructora e Ingeniería Sanitaria* (circa 1975) of the Ministry of Health and Assistance – SSA or the *Manual de Autoconstrucción y Mejoramiento de la Vivienda* (1984) by the National Autonomous University of Mexico – UNAM with the support of the Mexican company Cementos Tolteca. When both documents were published, the Spanish translation of the book *Architecture for the Poor* was already available. It was published for the first time in 1969 in a limited edition by the Egyptian Ministry of Culture, under the title *Gourna: A Tale of Two Villages* by the architect Hassan Fathy. Studies on collective or individual cases of professional practices were gradually added to these decades' production. For example, three volumes of *Hacia una teoría del proyecto arquitectónico* (2013) by Carlos González Lobo (1939-2021); *Oscar Hagerman Arquitectura y Diseño* (2014), as well as Mexican magazines such as *Código*. Number 82 (August-September 2014) of *Código* included articles such as "New challenges of social architecture", clearly influenced by *Talca cuestión de educación* (2013) and Harvard Design Magazine 34 (2011) dedicated to the Architectures of Latin America.

These triggered publications such as *Ciudades Radicales, un viaje a la nueva arquitectura latinoamericana* (2015) by Justin McGuirk or *Radical 50 arquitecturas latinoamericanas* (2017) by Miquel Adrià and Andrea Griborio.

The Contemporary Architect

In the 2016 congress Architecture: Climate Change, held in Pamplona (Spain), the Dutch architect Rem Koolhaas, who for decades has intervened in the architectural discipline through the media – now digital –, forming a large group of followers around the world, highlighted that the challenge of contemporary architecture is to understand the rural world.[3] This seems to belatedly encourage an analysis plan for the rural conditions under which millions of people live and from there justify the intervention of the contemporary architect. This rural life scenario is very interesting. Although it features extreme poverty, the lack of resources and Western industrial technologies make it possible to use other creative strategies that arise from living on the edge, on the periphery of modern technology, those that have been studied and cataloged as the collective intelligence that makes up community knowledge.

However, Koolhaas takes a step further, with the authority and arrogance of an architect, when he said at the same congress "we must think of methodologies for a landscape that sooner or later we will have to take care of [...] intervene in bare, semi-abandoned, poorly populated, sometimes poorly connected spaces."[4] This will be the proposal for the contemporary social agenda that the controversial architect Koolhaas discovered in his interest in the rural condition. A few months later, Chilean architect Alejandro Aravena was awarded the Pritzker Prize for his work on the Monroy farm in Iquique (Chile) which, after a few years, already shows signs of exhaustion in his promised and publicized social vitality.

These comments that the important and always listened-to-architect made from the comfort of an auditorium will resonate in different areas of architecture for communities. This call for a rural world crusade will have different fronts of new-generation architects, who connected in a global network, will find in their countries an opportunity for rural and community projects, and thus follow this contemporary route. In 2012, four years before Koolhaas' intervention, Australian architect Rory Hyde wrote *Future Practice. Conversations from the Edge of Architecture*, a book in which he proposes a reconfiguration of the architect's professional profile in the face of this complex world inserted in different anthropic crises: economic, environmental, social, etc. Hyde quotes John Thackara, for whom designers must "evolve from being individual authors of objects or buildings to becoming the facilitators of change among large groups of people."[5]

In this sense, we should also remember the controversial and not well-received book by Victor Papanek,[6] *Diseñar para el mundo real: ecología humana y cambio social* (Design for the Real World: Human Ecology and Social Change) (1970), whose author proposed to understand the design profession from a critical and ethical perspective, not necessarily complacent with what is established by cultural hegemony. The recurrent call to review and change the general designer's profile, particularly in architecture, suggests this possibility as an emerging symptom in crisis and vulnerability situations, which can be naively considered as a short cyclical process. Rather, we have the opportunity to analyze the theoretical and practical proposals of the necessary academic reconfiguration, especially in those latitudes where the crisis is a form of daily life adaptability.

Hyde's contribution in proposing new designer roles is important, each of them representing a future for the design practice based on its social potential. Hence, the contemporary designer in architecture, already far from those Vitruvian recommendations, can be reshaped as a community enabler, disciplinary integrator, social entrepreneur, visionary pragmatist, practicing researcher, long-term strategist, design management thinker, or unsolicited architect. Each of these new skills requires a willingness towards changing roles in the social sphere, and consequently, of those involved in learning and teaching architectural design.

However, this determination for the social-architectural has a long history in Mexico, at least since the third decade of the twentieth century: from the projects and works of Juan Legarreta (1902-1934) and Juan O'Gorman (1905-198), where a way of intervening in the country's social situation through the free professional exercise arises. In this recognition of new directions for architectural practice, the emergence of the academic dissidence of the auto-government within the Architecture School at the National Autonomous University of Mexico is fundamental. It is in the classrooms where the theory and project professors direct the student's efforts to get involved in the other reality of the country, especially within communities outside of the government's architectural and urban solutions.

This advancement by the university not only achieved social architectural projects at different scales but also more importantly, formed generations of architects with a critical and participatory outlook of the practice within the national territory and through its subsequent integration into the country's architecture schools. Examples of this social work were developed by Enrique Ortiz Flores, Oscar Hagerman, Carlos González Lobo, María Eugenia Hurtado, Valeria Prieto, José María Gutiérrez, Gustavo Romero and Isadora Hastings, or the German Anna Heringer and Ursula Härting. The early twenty-first century architects continue to work on this line of collaborative action via their architectural practices and through their direct or indirect influence on public or private universities. Although it can be understood as a generational change, it is part of a global and regional collective, where vitality lies in the formation of collaborative networks via courses, conferences, publications, competitions, awards, and projects that diversify its influence and confluence with the nowadays hyper-connectivity.

Works

Although talking about a set of works has the risk of choosing and therefore ignoring important cases, this selection highlights the fundamental theme worked at the beginning of the twenty-first century in Mexico, community spaces. We believe that the most important collective contributions of this generation and the frame of reference for the coming decades in Mexico and Latin America are found during this period. For this purpose, six architectural community actions carried out in the second decade of the twenty-first century were chosen (although others were observed), outlining the social work in the country. The selection comprises projects and works carried out in the states of Baja California Norte, San Luis Potosí, Oaxaca, Chiapas, Estado de México, and Puebla, acknowledging that similar projects that must be registered and analyzed have been developed in the rest of the country.

Oaxaca

A state in south-eastern Mexico, Oaxaca is characterized by a high level of poverty and a lack of economic projects encouraging social change. Within the 570 municipalities that comprise the state, in Zaachila there is a population within its southern mountain range called Pensamiento Liberal Mexicano, which is part of the municipality of San Miguel Peras with approximately 600 inhabitants. In 2012, community action was implemented here between the Faculty of Architecture at the National Autonomous University of Mexico (Max Cetto and Carlos Leduc Montaño workshops), the Italian collective Archintorno (working with the Politécnico de Torino in international cooperation projects), and the Centro de Apoyo al Movimiento Popular Oaxaqueño – CAMPO (Support Centre for the Oaxacan Popular Movement). The project and construction comprised designing a micro-regional center for sustainable technologies for the town. The architectural space aimed to concentrate the production and sale of fruit preserves to improve the precarious families' economies.

The project was developed in six months and constructed in three months, with the participation of the community and Mexican and Italian students. The work responds to its context by using local materials. The rectangular stone foundation protrudes from the ground to protect the rammed earth walls that form the ground floor – kitchen and sales room. The first floor comprises a wooden structure for the production workshop. The lightness of the wood is emphasized with different elements – boards, beams, columns, slats. The gable roof is formed by a wooden structure with an insulating layer of tejamanil, which is a wooden board characteristic of this area, and covered with zinc roof sheets, providing enough height to move the hot air out of the space. The wooden external staircase sits on the right side of the building. Likewise, a wooden mezzanine at the front protects the access from the sun and rain.

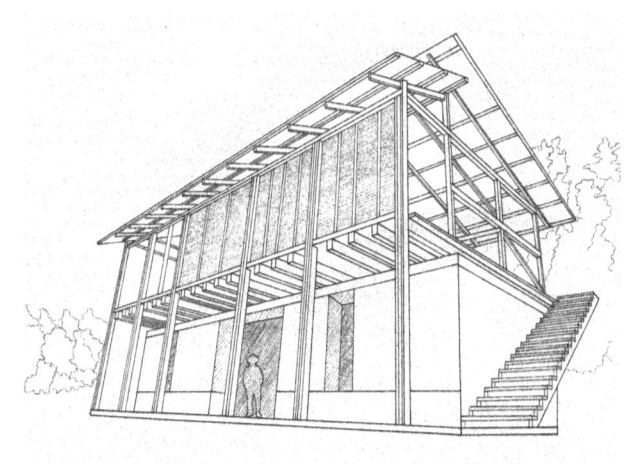

Perspective of the micro-regional Center for sustainable technologies, Oaxaca.

Source: José Francisco González Martínez, CAPUAO Archivo/FADU-UABJO, 2021.

As there is no built environment where the micro-regional center is located, the integration with nature is unbeatable, because the earth and wood generated a formal, volumetric, and spatial solution of contemporary quality. Over the years, the wood will take a patina that will change its perception. The slenderness of its double columns, separated from the ground by concrete and metal bases, as well as the blinds in the bordering corridor on the top floor, remind us of the principles of Japanese vernacular architecture. This work was part of Mexico's Pavilion "Despliegues y Ensambles" at the 15th International Architecture Exhibition of the Biennale di Venezia (2016), curated by Aravena.

Tijuana

On the northern border of Mexico, the city of Tijuana is a place for the confluence of bordering cultures, but also for problems of socio-urban overcrowding generated by immigration, which increases violence in peripheral colonies.[8] In December 2012, one of these colonies, known as Camino Verde, began a project to recover citizens' trust through an initiative by the organization Tijuana Innovadora, which was leaned a building by the Secretary of Social Development – Sedesol in the Federal Government. The organization implements the project and construction of the Casa de las Ideas (Ideas House), whose mission is

> [...] to be a community center that facilitates educational, artistic and cultural processes for children and youth as a strategy to prevent violence and crime in the city of Tijuana, with a sense of responsibility, empathy and solidarity [...] and whose vision is to contribute to the construction of citizen security, bringing the new generations alternatives that allow them to grow up with attachment to non-violence, culture of peace and respect for human rights.[9]

This project required a specific program of uses to detonate the proposed actions; hence, the Casa de las Ideas has 220 square meters to integrate workshops, a consulting area, an outdoor space for 120 spectators, and a digital library.

The site was crossed by a water canal on its longitudinal axis, which was piped. This axis was decisive in uniting the housing and commercial sides, with a project developed by CROstudio, a studio formed by architects Adriana Cuéllar and Marcel Sánchez. With a radical volume that contrasts with popular housing, this is an urban piece with a high-impact social program, becoming an extension of community life through multiple activities. Its border is permeable, so it directly interacts with the population. It has a functional plan, where elevation uses the volume of the digital library to create an outdoor space in which the topography becomes a platform. Its "wedge" shape is reminiscent of the auditoriums in Russian constructivist architecture (1920-1930).

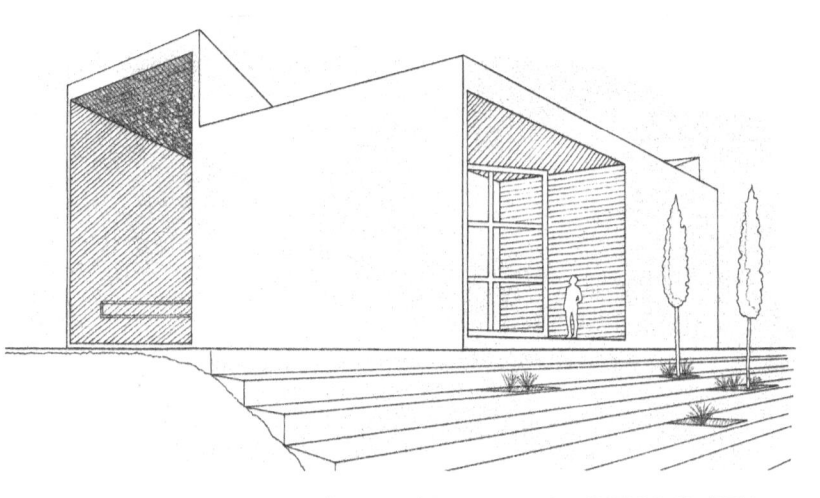

Casa de las Ideas (Ideas House), Tijuana
Source: José Francisco González Martínez, CAPUAO Archivo/FADU-UABJO, 2021.

This formal exploration creates a stage for music, theater, cinema, dance, etc. The Casa de las Ideas, an intervention scaled by a limited architectural program, is an example that social infrastructure in peripheral urban areas is possible with the efforts of stakeholders such as non-governmental organizations, neighbors, cultural promoters, government agencies, and, of course, architects with a vocation for community service. However, since the beginning of the twenty-first century, a cross-border cultural dynamic has been brewing in Tijuana by artists and architects who have developed specific and early actions between San Diego and Tijuana. For example, the Centro Cultural Tijuana - CECUT - in 1982 by architect Pedro Ramírez Vásquez (1919-2013), the participation in the International Fair of Contemporary Art ARCO'05 (held in Madrid, Spain, from February 8 to April 10, 2005) with the exhibition "Tijuana Sessions", and the Torolab collective work from 1995, founded by architect Raúl Cárdenas Osuna. Likewise, the cross-border research work by Guatemalan architect Teddy Cruz – architecture and urbanism professor from the Department of Visual Arts at the University of California, San Diego – and the recent opening of the Escuela Libre de Arquitectura,[10] which focuses on the formative practice of young architects.

San Luis Potosí

The Ejido Las Margaritas, 550 kilometers from the city of San Luis Potosí – the capital of a state with the same name –, is characterized by a desert landscape, with a lack of water resources. Therefore, the social conditions of its inhabitants, heirs of the sacred environmental culture of Wirikuta, are limited. In this context, between 2012 and 2013 the Comunidad de Aprendizaje, Dellekamp Arquitectos, and the Taller de Operaciones Ambientales – TOA (Environmental Operations Workshop) developed a project through participatory workshops with the Wirarika people to determine the objectives and uses for the social center to be designed and

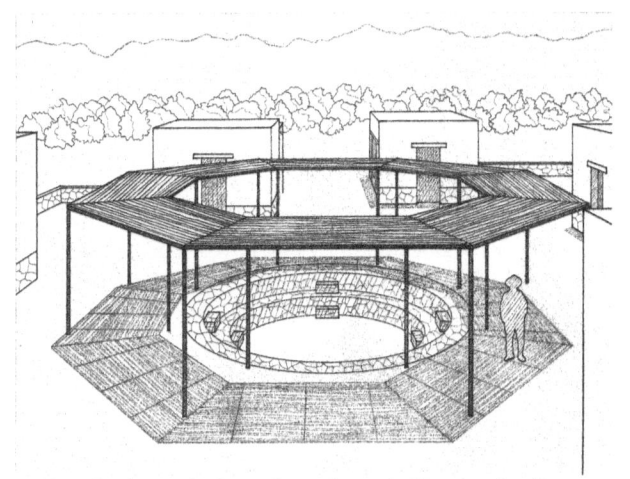

Las Margaritas Community Center, San Luis Potosí

Source: José Francisco González Martínez. CAPUAO Archivo/FADU-UABJO, 2018.

built. This resulted in a commission for a building to accommodate a meeting and events room, a natural products store for the Flor del Desierto women's cooperative, an internet center and library, as well as workshops and a garden.

The architectural proposal prioritizes the use of local constructive systems and materials such as stone, adobe, and wood, in tune with the reduction of the environmental impact. Therefore, the scheme is formed by independent functional volumes, which can be built in stages. A swastika shape organizes the program using rectangles with flat roofs and different dimensions but at the same height as the surrounding houses. Using spaces with variable dimensions in an asymmetrical site creates a dynamic perception, in which the roof of the greater volume is turned into a viewing platform.

This way of grouping the volumes serves as a defense against the prevailing winds, so the wall over the openings is a design feature. Given the climatic conditions and the permanent and extreme sunlight, it was necessary to

integrate a system of slender shading devices built with
a metal structure and natural fibers, which connects the
isolated pavilions protecting the circulations. In the center,
there is a circle that generates a sunken micro-space
protected by an octagonal cover and a bench to allow
community meetings. This small but dominant piece –
around which the volumes are arranged – highlights the
sense of community that gave rise to the ejido (communal
space) and is a daily reminder of ancestral ways used for
people to listen, organize, and discuss their proposals to
improve their living conditions.

Chiapas

In the country's southeast, within the state of Chiapas (next
to Oaxaca), the faculty of architecture of the Autonomous
University of Chiapas – UNACH – developed a project for the
elderly (2016) whose physical vulnerability is increased by
their social vulnerability, generating systemic isolation and
abandonment. This effort was promoted by the civil association Integralia Humanitaria and UNACH students. This care
module for the elderly and children in vulnerable situations is
the first part of a comprehensive project in the municipality
of Chiapa de Corzo, 20 minutes from the state capital city,
Tuxtla Gutiérrez. After a Construction Workshop exercise, a
proposal was chosen for development, management, and
implementation. A fundamental strategy was the use of
materials such as discarded brick from the site or from artisanal brick factories, as well as wooden doors and windows.
This practical exercise integrated the Domotej technology
into the roof, developed years ago by Dr. Gabriel Castañeda
Nolasco, professor and researcher of this architecture faculty.

The materials used in the development of this project
influenced its elementary planimetry, based on a dominant
rectangle with multiple uses and an adjacent rectangle for
the health service. However, these limitations were overcome
by the materiality achieved in the walls, lattices, floors, and

roofs. It was precisely the irregularity of the material that produced a singular expressiveness, which has been tested by the Paraguayan architect Solano Benítez and Argentine Rafael Iglesia. This constructive honesty reflects the harshness of a social project in governmental abandonment. La *Casa del Abuelo*, as this project is known, has taken part in recent South American biennials, capturing with its expressive rudeness the attention of researchers, teachers, and students. It emphasizes the willpower of young Chiapas students in small-scale social interventions suitable for the university level.

La Casa del Abuelo
(Grandfather's House), Chiapas
Source: Antonio Nivón, 2016.

Puebla

This was a small-scale architectural object that materialized in the medium term after the emergency caused by the earthquake of September 2017 with a magnitude of 8.2 on the Richter scale. It instigated the immediate response of students and professors of studio course VI at the Department of Architecture, Iberoamerican University (Puebla campus), who designed the San Juan Pilcaya Community Centre, in a rural community located 142 kilometers from the state capital. This project was made possible by the link between the Puebla Bambú group, the Institute of Design and Technological Innovation – IDIT at the Iberoamerican University, and the studio course VI (autumn 2017). Although the intention was to build bamboo housing

Infosismo, Puebla.
Source: Luis Moctezuma, 2018.

prototypes, economic limitations prevented its execution, so it was decided by the inhabitants to design a community center comprising three modules articulated around a square. The first was for post-earthquake social care, the second was for aid collection and distribution, and the third as a workshop to raise awareness of traditional construction techniques. Only this last volume was built, due to extreme limitations of economic resources, using wood, reed, earth, zinc sheets, and bahareque walls.

This pavilion rises above the natural terrain level, using concrete based on plastic buckets, as proposed by Shigeru Ban in his various prototypes of emergency housing. The 37 square meters' space completed in 2018 allows diversity of collective uses for the inhabitants of San Juan Pilcaya. This is architecture with scarce resources but of strong presence, since it not only differs in the place but is an example of what is possible to achieve with techniques and materials leveled by a perception of subdevelopment. This link between students, teachers, and San Juan's inhabitants is still active through three rural housing projects to be built.

Communal and social habitat

From the experiences presented so far, the socially responsible practice by the Taller Comunal stands out. Founded by Mariana Ordóñez Grajales (Autonomous University of Yucatan) and Jesica Amescua Carrera (Iberoamerican University), they have created a vision and mission of community architecture as the axis of their professional practice. Their actions are framed in favor of community projects closely related to what has been called *the production and social management of habitat*, in the last decades of the twentieth century, whose indefatigable promoter is the architect Enrique Ortiz Flores. For Mariana and Jesica, the value of the architectural project lies in being the representation of social processes of negotiation through agreements and solving normal disagreements. They conceive

[...] architecture not as a work of authorship, or as a static, artistic and unchangeable object, but as a collaborative, living, open and constantly evolving social process that allows the inhabitants to express their ideas, needs, and aspirations, always recognizing them as the center of projects' decision-making.[11]

The *Taller Comunal* has established itself as an emerging voice in the social practice of architecture, not only for its projects and awards obtained in Mexico, Latin America, Spain, and Portugal but also because it has defined its collaborative work under theoretical and epistemological premises. It is a workshop that has positioned its disciplinary action in tune with the discussion of socially relevant issues, such as the participation of women, human rights, the people's knowledge and self-determination, racism, colonialism, and technocracy. Therefore, the workshop incorporates a series of programs within its projects where they address the production and social management of housing, education, culture, and traditional knowledge, the social reconstruction of habitat, territorial understanding and memory.

Within the *Taller Comunal*'s portfolio, its relationship with the Tepetzintán community, in the north-eastern highlands of Puebla, has generated three important actions. There were two housing prototypes, one in 2013 and another in 2016, which instigated the third action, the design and construction of a Rural Productive School in 2018 to which we will refer. The absence of educational centers at the baccalaureate level for the community caused young people to stop their studies and interrupt their academic training. For this reason, and because of the experience with housing prototypes, young people decided to design and self-build the facilities of the Bachillerato Rural Digital number 186.

The construction of the first stage, comprised of two classrooms and services, was achieved with community input, providing local materials – bamboo, stone, and earth –, the workforce of young people, and the donation of the

Productive rural school, Puebla
Source: Onnis Luque, 2016.

land. During the construction and thanks to self-management, they gave alternative workshops to preserve traditional knowledge and trades. Formal logic determined the design of the classroom, favoring suitable lighting and ventilation, using a light roof construction with bamboo trusses and zinc sheets. These roofs are projected onto the longitudinal walls where the access is located. A corridor casts shadows on the door and windows, which fold to their full height between the foundation and the concrete beam that receives the roof trusses. Integrating a participatory design project, built with available materials and via social construction, has generated a practice of architecture from and for the community, strengthening affective ties and commitment, where architecture is a component of solidarity in Tepetzintán.

Final thoughts

These recent examples of community architecture in rural and urban populations in Mexico show the consistency of the projects originating from a genuine concern and vocation in intervening responsibly within the social scenarios around different crisis modalities. Participants faced constraints regarding time, place, resources, policy, and management. However, the sustained impulse exhibits a willpower for pragmatic and operational optimism (operational optimism in architecture OPOP), of which Manuel Gausa from Spain wrote about in 2005. In Latin America, it is in these strategies that the paradigm of solidarity underlies, because as Ana Patricia Montoya affirms:

> [...] these practices "are directly related to the presence of small community groups in urban and rural poor areas, with the idea of improving the quality-of-life of their inhabitants [...] thus, the idea of solidarity as a social value in a community implies, in the architectural field, an ethical problem directly related to the attitude

of the architect towards the profession and the production of work in relation to its local contexts.[12]

We propose to observe and characterize this architectural performance framework of third nature, following Hannah Arendt's book *The Human Condition,* and the three fundamental activities of the *vita active*: *labor, work, and action.* For these three foundations of the human condition to exist, they must be developed in a territory with appropriate characteristics for its transformation. This is changed from the first primitive nature, where there is no human intervention, into *alternum nauturam* or second nature with anthropic involvement and Arendt's *labor and work.* Finally, *action* is established when humans use their faculty in plurality, in the collective, and in politics. The so-called *third nature* belongs to this human condition, as *terza natura* that although "[...] refers to the concept of garden, it transcends the sense of the cultural landscape, because it is a space that is outside a utilitarian sense, consisting of an eutopia"[13] about solidarity.

This third nature is conceptually juxtaposed with Arendt's concept of *plurality* because it is

[...] the basic condition of both action and discourse that has the dual character of equality and distinction. If men were not equal, they could not plan and foresee the needs of those who would come later, if men were not different, that is, each human being differentiated from any other that exists, has existed, or will exist, they would not need discourse or action to understand each other.[14]

This would mean that the human transformation of the natural territory must be based on labor and work to turn it into *alternum nauturam* or alternate nature. From here only action in plurality becomes the third nature or *terza natura,* as the condition that transforms utopia into eutopia. A key element of this different stage of the crisis is being defined by the increasing emergence of eutopic[15] sociocultural acupunctures in Mexico and Latin America. According to Rory Hyde:

> [...] there are designers all over the world who are greedily forging opportunities for new forms of participation and collaboration, new types of design practices and results, and thus overturning the assumptions inherited from the design professions, to shape the adaptive action of making architecture in solidarity contexts.[16]

Notes

1. Quoted in Ramírez, Germán. "Las casas patio de Mies van der Rohe: un jardín de la modernidad. Una lectura desde el concepto de pluralidad y desde la tercera naturaleiza." *Dearq*, no. 19 (2016): 140-145, 141.
2. Hyde, Rory. "El futuro de la profesión." *Arquine*, no. 56, dosier 6 (2011).
3. Mora, Pola. "Rem Koolhaas en #CambioDeClima: 'el actual desafío de la arquitectura es entender el mundo rural." *Archdaily*, June 29, 2016 <https://www.archdaily.mx/mx/790455/rem-koolhaas-en-number-cambiodeclima-el-desafio-actual-de-la-arquitectura-esta-en-entender-el-mundo-rural>.
4. Ibid.
5. Thackara, John. *In the Bubble: Designing in a Complex Word*. Cambridge (Massachusetts): The MIT Press, 2005, 7.
6. Designer, anthropologist, writer and teacher, Victor Papanek (1927-1998) was born in Vienna (Austria) and emigrated to the United States in 1932, where he graduated in architecture and design at the Cooper Union in New York and completed postgraduate studies at the Massachusetts Institute of Technology – MIT.
7. Unpublished presentation by the authors for the XVII Seminar of Latin American Architecture (Quito, 2018), in which 2004 was identified as the date for the first projects under the international co-participation model in Oaxaca.
8. A mandatory reference to understand the context of Tijuana, are the observations of Monsiváis, Carlos, and Heriberto Yépez. Tijuana Sessions. Mexico City: Universidad Nacional Autónoma de México / Conaculta, 2005.
9. *Tijuana Innovadora* <https://tijuanainnovadora.org/>.
10. For more details about the free school of architecture, consult <www.ela.edu.mx>.
11. *Comunal Taller*. "Nosotras" <https://www.comunal-taller.com/nosotras>.
12. Montoya Pino, Ana Patricia. "Solidaridad." In *Ethos de la arquitectura latinoamericana: identidad, solidaridad, austeridade*, edited by Inés del Pino Martínez, 68-71. Quito: Pontifica Universidad Católica de Ecuador, 2018, 68.
13. Ramírez, "Las casas patio de Mies van der Rohe," 142.
14. Ibid., 143.
15. Eutopia comes from two Greek words: *eu*, which can be translated as adequate, good, convenient, or happy, and *topos* as place. It is a way of giving positive and achievable value to the word utopia that, on the other hand, would be a dystopia.
16. Hyde, "El futuro de la profesión," 2.

Post Scriptum
Babbling in Latin American Architecture of the 21st Century
Ingrid Quintana-Guerrero

Six months passed between writing these last lines and finishing the manuscript *Divergences,* in January 2022, which almost coincided with the end of the third millennium's second decade. Some texts presented address argumentative tendencies developed in a diffuse period of transition between the two centuries. Yet, twenty years is already a reasonable path to declare the twenty-first century as fully established intellectually and to observe, with sufficient detachment, phenomena in architectural thought that mutates vertiginously. In fact, six months seems already enough to observe the emergence of new milestones and paradigms in Latin America in the overlap of two centuries! These phenomena will be the input for the architectural discourses to be developed in the next five years. Here, I examine some of them based on the discussions previously raised in the book.

Foremost, the laudable effort to consolidate a Latin American theory by a group of academics and thinkers of architecture in the 1980s and 1990s – most of them affiliated with the Seminars of Latin American Architecture – SAL – has not had the long-lasting and far-reaching impact that they longed for on the subsequent architects' generations. Paradoxically, in the collective imagination, much of the 1980s intellectual production committed to the construction of regional identity has been associated with the vices of local architectural historiography. This has been identified by some critics and academics as an instrument of perpetual colonialism that architectural practice has intended to eradicate. This position is clearly exemplified by Felipe Hernández work: he highlights a fascination with the genealogies of the Modern Movement in Colombia, resulting in a narrative that seeks to take part in Eurocentric accounts, particularly in two fundamental works by Silvia Arango. "The point she continues to miss is that modern architecture is a 'knowledge', not simply a formal repertoire of urban and architectural forms to which one can contribute some."[1] I consider Hernández's criticism of Silvia Arango's works correct but unfair regarding the pioneering research that both Arango and other researchers of the same generation still carry out, aiming to study horizons different to modern architecture. It is also naive, as it ignores the imminent coexistence and eventual mutual inference of realities emerging from both sides of the Atlantic, announced in the introduction to this book. Contradictorily, Hernández echoes Walter Mignolo's call to avoid completely ignoring the contributions of a Western epistemology in the construction of his own thought. "Decolonizing Western epistemology means to strip it out of the pretence that it is the point of arrival and the guiding light of all kinds of knowledge. In other words, decolonizing knowledge is not rejecting Western epistemic contributions to the world. On the contrary, it implies appropriating its contributions in order to then de-chain [them] from their imperial designs."[2]

Although the perception of perpetual colonialism in the Latin American architectural thinking is not entirely wrong, it unwittingly validates the minor place assigned to the intellectual production of Latin American architecture in contemporary schools (especially elite schools). It is reduced to a regional stylistic search, instilling students the aspiration for an often-harmful leadership, in which individual and global[3] prominence prevail over the apprehension of the architectural craft as an arduous collective task within a specific context. The danger of this trend is that their young voices will be those who, in a not-too-distant future, will be recognized internationally as leaders of regional architectural thought. This danger was pointed out in this book by Fabricio Lázaro and Edith Cota and by me when referring to practice thought "from the bottom up."

In contrast, radicalization in the socio-economic contextual understanding of our discipline is present in certain academic groups with accentuated political militancy. While the current generation's global clamour for decolonization, equity, and social justice caters to the perennial architecture commitments, less desirable parallel phenomena have undermined such movements. For example, the public cancellation culture (mainly within digital media), positive discrimination to the detriment of meritocracy, cultural appropriation (trivialization) and *tokenism* have subtly permeated architectural debate scenarios, uncritically importing complex Anglo-Saxon social and political agendas. The class, race and gender gaps continue to be greater in Latin America. However, it is necessary to preserve scenarios in which to think holistically about the urgencies of architecture from and for the south, without falling into the naivety and reductionisms typical of ideological fundamentalism. It is also necessary to promote scenarios to imagine an architecture that fulfils the basic right to human habitation, built using not only words and images but also territory and matter.

Finally, and as I argue in the text *Inmundo: Architectural Metaphors from the Edge of the World* (previous research associated with *Divergences*), studying regions such as the South American Pacific, Central America and less visible countries and provinces in the Southern Hemisphere is complex because of the absence of both first-hand records and structured analyses. This is symptomatic of second-scale colonialism in the core of regional architecture studies – conceived in the great capitals, mainly in more visible countries with canonical historiographies such as Brazil, Mexico, and Argentina. My last and most urgent call is to examine the emerging architectural production in these geographies not only by observing their attractive forms and technological innovations but also by considering their social relevance and cultural and environmental contribution. All these factors – resulting from attentive listening to communities, knowledge, and environments – can ultimately dictate the real global impact of the architecture born in Latin America.

Notes

1. Hernández, Felipe. "Modern Fetishes, Southern Thoughts." *Dearq*, no. 29 (2021): 40-53 <https://doi.org/10.18389/dearq29.2021.05>, 44; 46.
2. Mignolo quoted in Hernández, "Modern Fetishes, Southern Thoughts," 47.
3. This is a palpable trend along the subcontinent, with the transformation of middle and secondary education curricula in which regional history has less room. There is also scarcity of specific courses on Latin American theory and a reduction of Latin American studies in architecture undergraduate programmes. This finding resulted from multiple conversations I had with the Latinx chapter of Global Architectural History Teaching Collective – GAHTC, particularly during the second workshop "Nuestro Norte es el Sur" (Our North is the South). This virtual workshop, organised by professors Ana María León at the University of Michigan and Fernando Martínez Nespral at the University of Buenos Aires (December 5, 2020), reflected on architecture's history teaching in Latin America with a global approach.

Divergent Voices

This microseries of three episodes compiles several interviews conducted by Ingrid Quintana-Guerrero during the fieldwork for the Divergencias research between 2018 and 2020. Its production is straightforward, not aiming to provide final conclusions, but rather to spotlight a tool that helped identify trends and paradoxes in the discursive construction of architecture in Latin America over the last two decades of the previous century and the first of the current one.

To access, scan this QR code.
Audio and texts only available in Spanish.

Episode 1
"Construcción crítica del pensamiento" (Critical Construction of Thought)
Episode 2
"El discurso frente a la historia" (Discourse before History)
Episode 3
"Diálogos Interdisciplinarios" (Interdisciplinary Dialogues)

Script: Ingrid Quintana-Guerrero; María Paula González
Camera: Ingrid Quintana-Guerrero
Editing: María Camila Gómez / La Oficina ArqDis

Authors' Biographies

Edith Cota Castillejos
Architect from the Benito Juárez Autonomous University of Oaxaca – UABJO (Mexico) with a master's degree in architecture from the Autonomous University of Yucatan – UADY (Mexico), with a PhD at the UABJO. She has published in books and local and national journals, book chapters with UADY, Michoacan University of San Nicolás de Hidalgo – UMSNH, Metropolitan Autonomous University – UAM, Autonomous University of Guerrero – UAGro, Pontifical Catholic University of Ecuador – PUCE, and the University Centre of Architecture, Art, and Design at the University of Guadalajara – CUAAD. She has been a speaker at architecture and urbanism national and international conferences in Spain, Argentina, and Ecuador. She is a research professor in the Faculty of Architecture at the UABJO, where she teaches History of Architecture from Mexico and Oaxaca with emphasis on the twentieth and twenty-first centuries. She is also a member of the CA Architectural Urban Heritage in Oaxaca, XVI-XXI centuries.

Fabricio Lázaro Villaverde
Architect from the Benito Juárez Autonomous University of Oaxaca – UABJO (Mexico) with a master's degree in architecture from the Autonomous University of Yucatan – UADY (Mexico), with a PhD from the Autonomous University of Morelos – UAEM (Mexico). Member of Documentation and Conservation of Buildings, Sites and Neighbourhoods of the Modern Movement – Docomomo Mexico. Since 1997, he is a lecturer and research professor in the Faculty of Architecture at the UABJO and a member of the Academic Group Architectural Urban Heritage in Oaxaca, XVI-XXI Centuries. He has publications in journals and book chapters with Metropolitan Autonomous University – UAM, Autonomous University of Guerrero – UAGro, Michoacan University of San Nicolás de Hidalgo – UMSNH, the UADY, Revista Latinoamericana de Estudios Urbano Regionales – EURE (Latin American Journal of Urban Regional Studies), Pontifical Catholic University of Ecuador – PUCE and with University Centre of Architecture, Art and Design at the University of Guadalajara – CUAAD. He is also a member of the Observatory of Contemporary Latin American Architecture, as well as the Scientific Committee of the Forum of Modern Architecture History and Criticism.

Ivo Giroto
Architect from the State University of Londrina – UEL (Brazil), with a master's degree and a PhD from the Polytechnic University of Catalonia – UCP (Spain). Post-doctorate at the School of Architecture and Urbanism at the University of São Paulo – FAU USP (Brazil). From 2012 to 2016 he was Professor and National Coordinator of the Estacio de Sá University – UNESA (Brazil). From 2019-2020, Director of the Brazilian Association of Architecture Teaching and from 2021 to 2022, member of the General Secretariat for Documentation and Conservation of Buildings, Sites and Neighbourhoods of the Modern Movement – Docomomo São Paulo. He is a researcher of the Observatory of Contemporary Latin American

Architecture and the group Culture, Architecture, and City in Latin America. He has published articles in various journals in Brazil, Portugal, Argentina, and Chile and investigates issues related to urban culture and modern and contemporary architecture in Brazil and Latin America, with emphasis on the production of cultural facilities.

Ingrid Quintana-Guerrero
Architect from the National University of Colombia – UNAL (Colombia), with a master's degree in History of Architecture from the Paris 1 Panthéon-Sorbonne University (France), another master's degree in Criticism of Contemporary Culture from the Paris 8 Vincennes Saint-Denis University (France) and a PhD in Architecture and Urbanism from the University of São Paulo – FAU USP (Brazil). Currently she is an associate professor in the School of Architecture and Design at the University of Los Andes – ArqDis Uniandes (Colombia). She has co-curated exhibitions with international itinerancy, including *Bauhaus Reverberada*, *Ethos de la arquitectura latinoamericana* and *La obra arquitectura de Le Corbusier*, both in 2018. She has been awarded the International Honorable Mention in the History, Theory And Criticism category of the Pan American Architecture Biennial of Quito (Ecuador, 2018); the National Honorable Mention in the History, Theory and Criticism category of the Pan American Architecture Biennial of Quito (Ecuador, 2020); the Honorable Mention at the Colombian Biennial of Architecture and Urbanism (2020); the *Prix de La Recherche Patiente* (Fondation Le Corbusier, 2016); the Scott Opler Fellowship for Emerging Scholars (SAH, Chicago, 2017; Montreal, 2021; Pittsburgh, 2022); and the Documentation and Conservation of Buildings, Sites and Neighbourhoods of the Modern Movement – Docomomo International Scholarship (Tokyo, 2020), among others.

David Vélez Santamaría
Architect from the National University of Colombia – UNAL (Colombia) with a master's degree in Architecture, Criticism and Project from the Pontifical Bolivarian University – UPB (Colombia). He is a professor researcher of the School of Architecture and Design of the UPB in Theory and History of Architecture and the research line of Criticism and Project. He has been the coordinator of the master's degree in Architecture at the UPB and co-researcher in several projects regarding the dissemination and criticism of architecture, as well as in a project pedagogy research. He has taken part as a speaker in international events, such as 2013 International Committee for Documentation and Conservation of Buildings, Sites and Neighbourhoods of the Modern Movement – Docomomo Brazil and 2018 Seminars of Latin American Architecture – SAL. His publications include *Arquitectura, proyecto del* ámbito público (2019) and *La imagen en la primera arquitectura posmoderna* (2020).

Romano Guerra Editora

Editors-in-Chief
Abilio Guerra and Silvana Romano Santos

Editorial Board
Abilio Guerra, Adrián Gorelik, Aldo Paviani, Ana Luiza Nobre, Ana Paula Garcia Spolon, Ana Paula Koury, Ana Vaz Milheiros, Ângelo Bucci, Ângelo Marcos Vieira de Arruda, Anna Beatriz Ayroza Galvão, Carlos Alberto Ferreira Martins, Carlos Eduardo Dias Comas, Cecília Rodrigues dos Santos, Edesio Fernandes, Edson da Cunha Mahfuz, Ethel Leon, Fernanda Critelli, Fernando Luiz Lara, Gabriela Celani, Horacio Enrique Torrent Schneider, João Masao Kamita, Jorge Figueira, Jorge Francisco Liernur, José de Souza Brandão Neto, José Geraldo Simões Junior, Juan Ignacio del Cueto Ruiz-Funes, Luís Antônio Jorge, Luis Espallargas Gimenez, Luiz Manuel do Eirado Amorim, Marcio Cotrim Cunha, Marcos José Carrilho, Margareth da Silva Pereira, Maria Beatriz Camargo Aranha, Maria Stella Martins Bresciani, Marta Vieira Bogéa, Mônica Junqueira de Camargo, Nadia Somekh, Otavio Leonidio, Paola Berenstein Jacques, Paul Meurs, Ramón Gutiérrez, Regina Maria Prosperi Meyer, Renato Anelli, Roberto Conduru, Ruth Verde Zein, Sergio Moacir Marques, Vera Santana Luz, Vicente del Rio, Vladimir Bartalini

Nhamerica Platform

Editor-in-Chief
Fernando Luiz Lara

Ediciones Uniandes

Editor-in-Chief
Juan Camilo González
Editorial Board, School of Architecture and Design
Roxana Martínez, Daniela Atencio, Ingrid Quintana-Guerrero, Eliana Sánchez-Aldana, Mónica Pachón, Adriana Páramo

Universidad de los Andes | Monitored by the Ministry of Education. Recognition as a University: Decree 1297 of May 30, 1964. Recognition of legal status: Resolution 28 of February 23, 1949, Ministry of Justice. High-quality institutional accreditation, 10 years: Resolution 582 of January 9, 2015, Ministry of Education.

All rights reserved. Legally constituted exceptions aside, no part of this publication, including the cover design, may be reproduced, distributed, publicly transmitted or transformed by any means, electronic, chemical, mechanical, optical, tape recording or photocopy, without prior permission in writing from both the copyright holders and the Publisher. Infraction of the rights mentioned may constitute an infringement of intellectual copyright.

Romano Guerra Editora
Rua General Jardim 645 cj 31
01223-011 São Paulo SP Brasil
rg@romanoguerra.com.br
romanoguerra.com.br

Nhamerica Platform
807 E 44th st,
Austin, TX, 78751 USA
editors@nhamericaplatform.com
nhamericaplatform.com

Ediciones Uniandes
Carrera 1.ª n.º 18A-12, bloque Tm
Bogotá, Colombia
ediciones@uniandes.edu.co
ediciones.uniandes.edu.co

Latin America: Thoughts
Romano Guerra Editora
Nhamerica Platform
Management Coordination
Abilio Guerra
Fernando Luiz Lara
Silvana Romano Santos

Divergences, Architecture in Latin America and Discourses of the End of the Century
Editor
Ingrid Quintana-Guerrero
Authors
Edith Cota Castillejos
Ivo Giroto
Ingrid Quintana-Guerrero
David Vélez Santamaría
Fabricio Lázaro Villaverde

BRA + USA + COL 11

Editorial Staff
Abilio Guerra
Fernando Luiz Lara
Irene Nagashima
Silvana Romano Santos
Graphic Design
Dárkon V Roque
Translation
Carolina Rodríguez
David Stevenson
Translation Review
Beatriz Lara
Noemi Zein Telles

©Romano Guerra Editora
©Nhamerica Platform
©Ediciones Uniandes
©Universidad de los Andes (Colombia), Facultad de Arquitectura y Diseño
©Ingrid Quintana-Guerrero
1st edition, 2024

Cataloging-in-publication (CIP)
Câmara Brasileira do Livro, SP, Brasil

Divergences
Architecture in Latin America and
Discourses of the End of the Century
ed. Ingrid Quintana-Guerrero.

1st edition
São Paulo, SP: Romano Guerra
Austin, TX: Nhamerica Platform
Bogotá, CUND: Ediciones Uniandes.
2024

ISBN 978-65-87205-30-4

1. Architecture
2. Latin America - Environmental Aspects

I. Quintana-Guerrero, Ingrid.

24-200496	CDD-720

Indexes for Systematic Catalog
1. Architecture 720

Cover Image
Cemetery at Ciudad Abierta, Ritoque (Chile). Corporación Amereida, 1976-2002. Photo by Ingrid Quintana-Guerrero, 2019, edited by Darkon Roque.

Catalog sheet prepared by librarian
Tábata Alves da Silva - CRB-8/9253